Gay
Liberation
At a
Psychological
Crossroads

Gay Liberation At a Psychological Crossroads

A Commentary on the Future Of Homosexual Ideology And Establishment of the Institute For Contemporary Uranian Psychoanalysis, in Four Parts, Delivered in Honor of the Third Anniversary of the Institute

Mitch Walker, Ph.D.

Institute for Contemporary
Uranian Psychoanalysis

LOS ANGELES

ISBN-10: 1-4392-5402-8
ISBN-13: 978-1-4392-5402-8
Library of Congress
Control Number: 2009908288

Cover design by Chris Kilbourne
Book design by Roger Kaufman

Photo credit (p. 99): Tetraktys

Institute for Contemporary
Uranian Psychoanalysis
P.O. Box 931347
Los Angeles, CA 90093

Visit www.amazon.com to order additional copies.

PREFACE

This is the published version of a four-part public presentation delivered between January and May of 2009 at Plummer Park, West Hollywood, California. Each talk was preceded by an introductory section, and in this printed version, these preliminary remarks have been consolidated into a general Introduction to the entire series. Also, references cited in the text are now listed at the back, along with a few referrals to basic books in the areas of Jungian psychology, Gay Liberation and its history, and the modern development of subjectivity, for the interested reader who would like to learn more about these topics. In addition, I should mention that an interesting question and answer period followed each delivery which will not be reproduced in the current work but which may become available at the website of the Institute for Contemporary Uranian Psychoanalysis, www.uranianpsych.org. I have also included in an addendum a related short commentary I more recently gave at another Institute educational event on topics similar to those taken up in my four-part discussion. Except for minor adjustments, the text of each talk has been preserved as originally delivered for the sake of its accurate documentation as such. For further inquiries, please contact the Institute at P.O. Box 931347, Los Angeles, CA 90093, (323) 692-9336 or info@uranianpsych.org.

Mitch Walker
August 2, 2009

TABLE OF CONTENTS

INTRODUCTION

Greetings. My name is Mitch Walker, and I am the principal co-founder of and advisor to the Institute for Contemporary Uranian Psychoanalysis, the first homosexually-centered psychoanalytic research and training facility, which is now in its fourth year of operation. Actually, I have been serving in this way "behind the scenes," so to speak, for more than eleven years, as the early, pre-Institute public talks then being given by Chris Kilbourne and Doug Sadownick—which themselves had taken over from an even earlier series I had been offering—have since developed into the better articulated formats being seen today and into the future. Therefore, it marks a significant shift in my participation in the Institute to address you directly in this fashion, one motivated by a growing interest to become more actively involved in Institute educational efforts.

As someone who could be thought of as a "gay tribal elder" in our homosexual community, to use a currently popular phrase, I am in that capacity feeling a growing pull or moral "call" to share my life experiences, views, and sensibilities in accessible forms of interpersonal public exchange, due to what seems to me to be an expanding community need and readiness for such seasoned people as myself, and for the sorts of specific considerations I will detail in my comments below.

To inaugurate this expanded activity, I have prepared some remarks called "Gay Liberation at a Psychological Crossroads: A Commentary on the Future of Homosexual Ideology and Establishment of the Institute for Contemporary Uranian Psychoanalysis, In Four Parts, Delivered in Honor of the Third Anniversary of the Institute," which consists of a revised and extended version of a two-part discussion offered last Fall.

With this four-part commentary, I will outline a perspective for considering current liberatory challenges and opportunities facing us, as gay and lesbian persons and a community, in relation to the founding of the Institute for Contemporary Uranian Psychoanalysis. This is not to imply, in regard to the organized same-sex-loving minority, that other kinds of identities, persons, or viewpoints are not important or valid here or elsewhere, only that I will be speaking as a gay-identified homosexual focusing on gay topicality and signification. I should also point out that I will be doing so as a *male* homosexual, therefore my comments will, in part, more aptly pertain to gay men, but I hope not to the exclusion of an equitable lesbian appreciation, and my apologies for the inevitable gender bias that is present in these remarks. It actually seems to me that Sapphic women's procreative possibilities may realistically be of even greater significance than those of their gay male peers, and I hope that in the future this sublime gynecoid potentiality can be increasingly directly explored and most richly activated.

I might also mention that I have chosen to prepare these remarks in writing beforehand and then read them to you here, not only to have the material well thought out and clearly documented in an easy distributive form, but moreso through such an appropriately-scripted opportunity, to somewhat queerly invoke rhetorically, with vigorous thought and sincere feeling, a powerfully-stimulative conception of gay psychological valuation provocatively unprecedented in conventional social discourse, and in so doing to accordingly undergo, with everyone here today, an important and meaningful public ritual, the witnessed incantational performance of that pioneering invocational statement.

Additionally, I should let you know that this talk will be pretty *intellectual*, in the sense of trying to consider and handle ideas seriously and responsibly, but not *too* seriously, I hope, and in that conscientious sense, the discussion will get fairly dense, even though I have tried to convey its ideational expression in plain English as much as possible. Nonetheless, due to this cumulative intellectual substantiality, it could be a little taxing to keep up with, so I will attempt to read the following statement with that in mind, in order to assist the thoughtful listener in better following along. This is also a major reason why we have provided you with a hard copy of the talk when you came in tonight, in case referencing it as I speak may additionally aid in its improved comprehension.

GAY LIBERATION AT A PSYCHOLOGICAL CROSSROADS: THE GOLDEN OPPORTUNITY TO BIRTH A HOMOSEXUALLY-CENTERED PSYCHOANALYSIS

It seems to me that the historical Gay Liberation Movement of actually the last century and a half, is today at a profound ideological and practical crossroads in terms of its greater future development and even its continued creative viability, due to the interlocking combination of its own growing success and the fierce persistence of homophobic forces traditionally deployed against it, and not only or even in the end most importantly as that terrible bigotry is still applied in meanspirited opposition to valuable homosexual realization by persons and ideologies external to gay people themselves, but even more importantly, as that ancient form of social scapegoating has been and is hurtfully impacting maturationally becoming and individually being meaningfully same-sex loving now.

The historic truthfulness of Gay Liberation—that there are and always have been individuals who are indigenously aligned erotically and romantically primarily to others of similar biological gender, that such people have the inherent right to respect, identify with, and live life out in terms of this compelling amatory alignment, and to appropriately develop shared values, cultures, and communities with others of like mind—the intrinsic validity of this progressive humanizational sensibility has finally led through great bravery, sacrifice, and persistence to increasing acceptance and comprehension by homosexuals of ourselves as such, to the dignificational personalization of being amorously same-sex oriented, and accordingly, to characterological achievement of today's integrated and empowering gay ego identity, one which can effectively engage with the world to meet sexual, romantic, and other basic interpersonal needs caringly, humanely, and satisfyingly. As this just and long-needed truthfulness has become better tangibly realized, homosexual folk have cultivated and fortified ourselves in supportive collective association to succeeding degrees of clarified self-definition that have revolutionarily transformed not only our own lot in life and that of our immediate successors, but as well affected the entire human world, increasingly so.

However, the loathsome sources of virulent homophobia have not in consequence been altogether rooted out, by any practical means, although our deservedly greater success in more-recent historical time, as individuals and a community, in reclaiming homosexual content and process for ourselves and the world, may deceptively make it seem as if the vile power of social bigotry had been successfully enough banished, particularly for oneself and for the immediate affinity of like-minded others. Thus, the brightness of our worthy achievements can also cast an obscuring shadow.

It is perhaps not then an obscure coincidence that the soothing doctrines of gay assimilationism now pretty much rule our community's dealings and formulations, and such ideologies accept homosexual identity on the basis that same-sex-loving peoples are otherwise and except for unjust social bigotry only different from everybody else in relatively minor ways, such as in terms of the gender that we do it with in bed, that in all essential ways such as the legal or moral, we are "just the same." And while it seems true to me that the ethical ideal of democratic equality is indeed fair and realistic, it is also true that its over-simplified acceptance can reduce or block appropriate appreciation of how homosexuality is not heterosexuality in some very profoundly-implicated ways, and how its proper individuation in people would accordingly proceed, not in an assimilating or homogenizing fashion, but rather in a "gay-centering" manner uniquely prospective and importantly contributive in its own distinct right. Thus, the strategic reign of gay assimilationist ideologies, in gaining their very sociopolitical successes, can also be promoting to that validational extent a paradoxical negation of what makes being gay gay for members of the concerned community otherwise benefitted, thereby fostering a discordant contradiction thus so sympathetic or helpful to the ugly forces of heterosexist hatred still working their nasty will on us, most acutely and dangerously as the Trojan Horse within, as persistent or deep-seated "internalized homophobia."

The unfortunate limitations of gay assimilationism, as well as the relentless pressures of conservative social attitudes generally, can be noted throughout the gay community today in concert with the tremendous losses we have suffered from AIDS. One may fairly observe a manifest decrease, in some ways, in homosexual community presence, vitality, and creativity, particularly in those metropolitan locales most successfully and long-lastingly "liberated" for same-sex-loving folk, as one manifestation of these inhibitory and corrosive factors not presently being sufficiently adequately dealt with. On the level of ideology, we can see by the relative sterility and stagnation of assimilationist-oriented gay liberation theory and practice in not being able to more powerfully address subjective homosexual growth after securely coming out as a crucial manumissional factor in our Movement's greatest-possible future success, that a much more serious level of comprehension is needed of *adult* homosexual personhood, its origins, composition, possibilities, oppression and freedom, in terms of a more-complete gay liberation.

In my experience, it is absolutely not the case that reconciling to one's same-sex-loving orientation and forging a "healthy gay identity" which is socially successful—although absolutely pivotal steps in appropriate self-empowerment—

resolve all or even the most poisonous influences of not only growing up alone in a hateful, alien world, homocentrically speaking, but on top of this, of having to ongoingly function as valuably homosexual vis-à-vis a social universe which is still vastly inhumanely biased against that. Thus, while the just gains we have made in integrating our sexuality and rejuvenating our self-definition are rightly to be celebrated and continuously confirmed and extended, these very achievements, particularly in the persistently-threatening context of powerful opposing forces, can help mask an equal necessity to then deal with deeper-seated internalized homophobic effects so as to reach a better and truer basis to be more-fully personally "liberated," empowered, realized, and satisfied as a self-respecting and progressively-oriented lesbian or gay human being in today's challenging world.

These concerns are ultimately or most aptly related to that knowledge domain called "psychology," by which I mean, first, a name for the encompassing realm of subjective human phenomena, and then, therapeutically based attempts to study, comprehend, and better engage that living but intangible reality, here, those efforts most prominently arising in the last hundred years from the ideological system called by Freud "psychoanalysis." Thus, experiences of sexual desire and romantic love are psychological in nature, genesis and operation of sexual orientation likewise occur psychically, and achievement of a gay identity similarly manifests as well, no matter what exterior factors or forces may have played a part historically or otherwise in that self-distinguishing manifestation.

I am talking here about the interior psychology of becoming, being, and growing over the lifespan as a worthy homosexual person today and into the future, both these discrete subjective phenomena themselves and their attempted psychodynamic comprehension. I am suggesting that as we cultivate such an insightful introverted appreciation in the developmental context of historical gay liberation, an intellectual recovery effort still just beginning after decades of homophobic prejudice in published psychological thinking, a more expansive perspective is revealed about homosexual psychological freedom and complete maturation that locates the worthy achievement of a secure gay identity as the auspicious start to an even more-profound phase in becoming fully personally same-sex loving, one that is best taken advantage of, where possible, so as to better thwart bigoted intentions and reach our superior actualizational possibilities, one that requires and produces a growing facility for that singular type of supportive or affirming psychic self-awareness by which the alchemy of enriching interior initiation and constitutional transmutation can best be appreciated and enabled homosexually.

This is the ideological and practical crossroads that the Gay Liberation Movement is at today, either to renew its mandate and deepen its import by seriously taking up a gay-centered psychological method, or to creatively stagnate in the face of continued oppressive forces within and without that bitterly oppose homosexuality and the successful cultivation of better psychological consciousness overall.

I say, let's become more homosexual, not less, by seeking enhanced initiatory relations with that force or presence in us instigative of good gay desire and romantic feeling to begin with, starting through honest, penetrating, and effortful psychological self-engagement affirmingly undertaken as we relate to others and live in the same-sex-loving community and the larger world. That is the purpose of cultivating a gay-centered psychology as the next stage of gay liberation theory and practice, and that is accordingly the reason for establishment of the Institute for Contemporary Uranian Psychoanalysis here in Los Angeles.

The concept of "Uranian psychoanalysis" refers to a progressive marriage of homosexually-centered valuation and psychoanalytic formulation that incorporates the already-established literature about homophobic trauma on good homosexual personality growth or "gay-affirmative" psychology into a prime conceptual extension to Jungian analytic thinking, a "Uranian" extension. This term refers to a well-known story in Plato's *Symposium* about same-sex love having a unique matron goddess, "heavenly" Aphrodite Urania, she who was born from her father's severed testicles fallen into the sea. Thus, the phrase "Uranian psychoanalysis" refers to the study and appreciation of what is *transpersonal* and *individuational* about being distinctly homosexual, in the Jungian sense, which is that of the profoundest reformational possibilities for psychological self-awakening as the golden shamanic road to fullest creative humanization.

How much more apt can that farsighted analytic sensibility be than as rightly applied to the comprehensive quest for complete gay liberation? Envision being a homosexual person in revealing terms of an inherent teleological intent authoritatively rising, as Jung might say, from the archetypal Self, the godly center and circumference of ultimate subjective existence in the ethical and spiritual sense. Picture gay desire as a personifying invitation by the psychological "soul" to a life-long love affair with deity that can progress thematically through inner stages of transformational fathoming in concert with outer affectional intimacy to the satisfying point of the richest qualitative realizations. Imagine same-sex romance as transpersonally summoning a promotional spirit of twinship mutuality which is at the very heart and essence of the dignifying human pursuit of equality, democracy, and individual justice in a peaceful, loving world.

The greater alchemical treasures of what C.G. Jung called the "collective unconscious" are made more accessible gradationally through a depthful analytic approach which rightly appreciates effortfully engaging one's shadow-side relationally for the sake of that obtainable numinous enrichment, or rather, grappling with how one is presently for the most part unwittingly entangled in one's shadow-side of past and present malevolently-hurtful forces, most so within the realm of one's *feeling* for oneself, as the beginning of an intensifyingly-purposeful creation of new psychological consciousness, a transmuting tincture and medium of accumulating potency and change that inevitably leads internally to increasingly integrated intimacy with subjectively manifesting sacrality.

Such a preeminent world of self-confirmation and moral deepening is available to growth-oriented gay and lesbian people through good cultivation of an authentic and affirming psychological attitude, an ennobling direction pragmatically in tune with that improved self-awareness involved in achieving a valued gay identity, and with what, from a depth perspective, can be homocentrically imagined to have inspirationally and directionally gotten us to become and be same-sex oriented originally, the primordial aboriginal Spirit of centralizing homosexual desire, what we could call divine Uranian Eros.

The Greek love god Eros was taken up by Jung as a metaphorical concept or symbolic representation of an inherent aspiration in the sexual urge toward reaching a greater wholeness, particularly internal wholeness, what Jung means by individuation or becoming a specific person. If we understand Uranian Eros as psychically behind the rise of homosexual desire, orientation, identity, thus history and community, then its additional intentions for same-sex-loving people are historically at the fecund point where more purposeful facilitation of gay self-becoming would prove most fruitfully useful. It must be the case that the overall effect of heterosexist oppression has been lessened significantly enough on overt homosexual being through all our dedicated struggles such that we can now attempt to reach beyond previous, homophobically-sourced limitations of good self-becoming and qualitative validation by forthrightly entering a new stage of psychologically-focused gay liberation thinking and parallel action that best supports, engages, and follows out the farther possibilities of entelechical Uranian Eros in salutary subjective humanization and its additional self-interested politicization through cultivating homosexual psychological awareness towards satisfactional fulfillment of a *second stage in gay identity formation*, the constructive alchemical fashioning of more-complete valuative self-realization in a preciously-distilled sense of interiorly-reformed gay personhood.

To give you a better sense of what this greater homosexual destiny of estimable self-becoming might amount to subjectively when pictured in a gay-centered psychological fashion, let me describe a possible comprehension of homosexual personality development from the perspective of relevant transpersonal themes as synthesized from gay liberation, psychoanalytic, and Jungian ideas. For the sake of greater specificity, I will focus on the psychology of gay men, although a parallel understanding would be equally available for lesbian women.

Imagine that in the beginning of personal existence, a primordial Essence, intrinsic to the basic life force, spontaneously emerges from the archetypal Self or preconceived idea of incarnating subjective being, an essential procreative seed that we can characterize figuratively as the original source and guiding "intelligence" of elementally flowing libido. Dynamic libido is the expressive energic agency of the individuation instinct or primordial urge to become an individual, and rousingly animates the variously-configuring symbols of substantiating transformation by which existent subjectivity factually occurs and valued personhood fruit-fully organizes and deepens. In most people who have devel-oped a secure personal sense of biological gender identity, that they are male or female, which usually occurs by around two years of age, the further channeling of fundamental libido into genital sexuality, and then adult romance, subse-quently "turns," at least mainly, in an opposite-gender-oriented amorous way, but in those persons who become immutably gay-identified, it turns systematically and vigor-ously in a same-gender aligning way, and so their basic vene-real libido is consequently organized homosexually. This defining same-sex expression in our imaginative formulation arises from, and is so directed by, the verdant Essence of all-possible subjective existence, which numinous cause is thus rightly regarded as the autochthonously enlivening Essence of meaningfully-demarcating gay eros, love, identity, language, and feeling life as most ethically worthy and spir-itually good achievements in developing self-creative per-sonhood's finest wholesome maturation. The beneficial actualization of primordial, vital Essence well gained psy-chologically through clarifyingly becoming successfully homosexual in amatory feeling and coherent thought is revealed by this interpretive line of depthful analytic reason-ing to be the premier formational route by which the cos-mogonic archetypal Self incorporationally individuates itself specifyingly in subjectively forming gay men.

The nifty evolutionary route through which the arche-typal Self brings about this most importantly valued realiza-tion of same-sex-loving actuality, would then consist, analogous to productive heterosexual development, as fair logic and unbiased perception would sanely suggest, initially in constellation of a homosexual Family Romance during the Oedipal stage of psychosexual growth. I have called this gay familial distillation of crucial object relations the Uranian complex: A forming gay boy is impelled by the primordial Essence to fall in love incestuously with his phallic father in order to maturationally fulfill the personality-building organization of his early genital striving through that meaningful patterning route, and in consequence he is well entrancingly drawn to heroically seek satisfying possession, at least in fantasy, of his yearned-for father's phallic love for him, by imaginally taking his mother's married place relationally to father, in what would then compose a homosexual form of crucial symbolic return to the founding Primal Scene, the sourceful parental act by which personal being first came into tangible existence. This same-sex incestuous metaphorical yearning to participatorily recreate one's own origin, attitudinally leads to an ambivalent identification with the figurative mother, whereby the contrasexual anima archetype in the psyche is not further split off from the nascent ego's accessible experience, as it would be in male heterosexual personality growth, even though that gay ego-to-be had previously securely attained a masculine gender identity clarifyingly separating it from the feminine, but relationally becomes instead an inner incorporating "body" of joyously felt desire, valuationally deep emotion, and substantively actualized composition as intelligibly personally homosexual, the capable psychic vessel of the buoyant thriving Heart nutritiously to be satisfied fulfillingly in natively-good gay love, which is increasingly aligned with consonantly by the consciously-emergent ego. And the archetypal image of the Masculine, which I am most fundamentally picturing allegorically as a figurative phallic double of one's own literally-perceived genitals, as that personified figure of the typic male sex which had earlier provided the analogical basis for a gay man to congruently identify with his own biological gender, is now properly infused excitationally with the numinously-ultimate *mysterium* of the transcendental relational "soul," the soul as a Jungian concept meaning the inner felt source of enlivening inspiration, particularly as most potently manifested in personified romantic form, what Jung means by his classic definition of a man's "anima."

By way of such metaphorical understanding, it can be appreciated that sexual orientation and romantic soul are not necessarily in their functioning particularity simply preordained by nor in merely automatic compensation for a person's biological gender or for a basic bodily identification congruently as a biological male or female, although such causal connections have been usually assumed in classical Jungian thought about human sexuality, but instead are more realistically considered to develop from their own autonomous factors at a later stage of compounding subjective growth in league with that previously-achieved biological identification. Thought out in this way, the basic figuration of the contrasexual gender, anima, can be appreciated to coalesce in the unconscious psyche of every man, yet it does not necessarily carry the central electrifying meaning of deepest soul arousal as provoked by a genitally-defining soul-figure, whereas alternatively, when the libidinal Essence Oedipally animates the phallic double, the personified iconic image of a man's own male gender also carried representatively in his unconscious, then it is in this twinning figurational pattern that the elemental genital soul transfixes him and seeks productive romantic union, first in compelling projected form. It is this amorous dioscourian image, then, that emblematically portrays his most aroused feelings and best passionate experiences of bewitching soul-possession, such that the responsive man, thus so fatefully grasped, initially becomes aware but dimly of this conforming emotive twin-soul in the incestuous childhood yearning for his father, and later, through the same helpful mechanism of libidinal transformative sublimation as also occurs to heterosexual boys, more clearly in the hotly-

stimulating forms of attractive men and their images as manifested through those diverse piquant variations of sexual and
romantic pattern pubescently emergent parallel to that
expressive range typically seen in adult heterosexuality. Yet
behind all these divinely-scrumptious homosexual soul-
images, as they appropriately concern the healthfully maturing
growth of psychic object relations and the unfolding symbolic
mystery of mutual romantic love in the respectful humanistic
way being thematically appreciated by this upright circumam-
bulating discussion, causally lies that entrancing archetypal
figure we have been here suggestively exploring, the vital
wraith-buddy soul, an awesomely-erotic male presence as the
personified magical twin to one's own penis, a mesmerizingly
attentive spirit-being, singularly attuned, electrifyingly lus-
cious, dazzlingly regal, beautifully different yet thrillingly mirroring, outrageously incestuous while verdantly nutritious,
whose doubly desired embrace is the mutually riveting experience of finest qualitative completion in treasurably-renewing
symbolic return to the all-possible Primal Source, whose
luminous sorcerous semen is the most procreative Dew of
heavenly incorporative attainment.

To encounter the personally activated double-soul in
such-like glorious amative fashion would be iconic and
ecstatic, it can be easily pictured, conveying an unrefusable
symbolic invitation in the radiant Eternal Heart to earnestly
climb a wondrously-accessing atomic ladder from elemental
Earth to superlative Heaven, and so live completionally with
a soul-twin also succulently thereby matured, forever distil-
lationally embodied in existent being's fine paradisal perfection. I recall that when I worked with Harry Hay in founding
the Radical Faerie movement in the late 1970s, he would
repeatedly and lyrically tell the story of his childhood dream
to find another boy like himself, and the two of them would
then walk hand in hand up a beautiful green hill to greet a

glorious sunrise. Is that not suggestive of the heavenly motif I was just describing?

Such an overwhelmingly heartfelt, transcendent invitation and its eagerly enthusiastic reply in young childhood, would then set in motion the "archetypal theme of romance" (Gardner & Maier, 1984, p. 40) as that life-long personal undertaking which depthfully reflects the genuine subjective gravity defining paramount gay love for gay people, the clarion call and responsive yearning to focally relate with this dazzlingly-customized heaven-likeness, and accordingly to be fully incarnately wedded productively in completing valuational partnership to him satisfyingly forever, an amorous tensional dynamic initiating in consequence a supreme heroic quest, "the search for the other self" (Fone, 1980, p. 9) and thereso its geminational metaphysical Source. The suchwise-chosen child, well-seduced by this masterfully rousing Romance, richly "inspired by the romantic ideals of homosexual love" (p. 10) with that utmost innocent sincerity as only young passion can be, will then most movingly attempt to climb an accessioning Divine Ladder in his thereby-transformable Sacred Heart, and to do so will capably usher him analogically into an alchemical "perilous journey" (Gardner & Maier, 1984, p. 40) conducted phenomenally within his evolving subjective being, by which route the goodly formation of a strong conscious ego and a meritorious gay identity will occur together self-directionally in the developmental context of a nutritively-embodying homosexual personhood of increasingly meaningful scope and enhanced substantiating depth.

When the intended gay-man-to-be, joyously first transfixed at the age of three, four, or five by the mesmeric calling of his ravishing Beloved in the mythic Uranian familial complex thereby becoming passionately well established, spiritedly reaches out to courageously start his stalwart climb on the sensational Divine Ladder to Heaven, he must of necessity grasp the hand of a dark lord as well as that of a light one, because it turns out that the metaphorical Divine Ladder is ruled over by oppositional twin gods, in ancient Egyptian thought most typically portrayed by the brothers Horus and Seth, and formidable Seth's contributing hand is a sticky mass of wriggling snakes, much as the later Greeks pictured serpentine Typhon, one of the giant Titans. By way of a young boy's hearty answer to the numinous call for homosexual romantic love, therefore, a Typhonian reversal twistingly occurs within the nascent subjective realm. The god-like inspirational yearning for utter romantic merger with the literal phallic father is inevitably thwarted by the forbidding incest taboo, which is also archetypally innate, and this developmentally-required failure accordingly transforms, instead of only eliminates, the dastardly incest wish into the viable basis for all later amatory yearnings, as that same libidinal change helps better constellate and strengthen a budding proto-ego already much advanced maturationally due to its initial incestuous wishing, so that it might better reach for its ultimate desirous goal through not only a feminine matrimonial motivic identification but one cohesively fortified even more by inevitable defeat in literally supplanting mother's place with father.

The germinating gay ego, thuswise developmentally supported and androgynously propelled, is cast down symbolically, in our imaginary exploration, into a subliminal confrontation with the fecund darkness of the unconscious over the now-shameful issue of genital meaning, as it grows in sensible coherence during the ensuing latency stage of psychosexual evolution, and so that differentiating ego must unknowingly enact the difficult combat of fraternal Horus and Seth. This subterranean allegorical struggle during the pre-pubescent years is the shapefully engaging mechanism for the farseeing double-soul's further effectuation of goodly subjective self-becoming, it has the character of an erotically charged but dangerous wrestling match, by which a nurturing give-and-take relationship with the needful unconscious through interior romantic bonding can be usefully established to the extent that such a hard-fought struggle can be sufficiently sustained. As the infernal underworld task is worked through subconsciously by way of this nutritious combat over Oedipal desire versus shame, a dewy resolutional Intelligence is eventually inseminated supernaturally and then embodied alchemically within the maturing child's inner Eternal Heart, a new guiding connection to something like primordially wise Thoth, Egyptian god of wisdom and realization, is well established there, and a divine greening Mystery of the combative Two Partners culminatingly reveals itself. Percipient Thoth brings about a reunion of the conflictual opposites in meaningfully growing psyche, there is a magical metamorphic reconciliation with the fractious unconscious, and then a most-precious birth in the dawn of coming pubescent enlightenment.

This entire sequence of sound personality development propels an unconscious childhood differentiation that prepares the way for coherent individual consciousness and adult emotional life. Now a newly expanded emergence of the ardent double-soul can occur with the stirring advent of waxing sexual adolescence, so as to confront the more-advanced proto-ego in a more conscious way with an echoing recapitulation of the initial invitation in the Sacred Heart, a rejuvenated reaching to stalwartly climb the heavenward Divine Ladder, now through romantic genital attraction to other males more generally, followed by another twisting Typhonian reversal additionally fed by having to live in a heterosexist, homophobic world. Again the intrepid personality, well supplied by the genuinely bottomless vigor of its most-heartful procreative calling, is nicely enabled to progress persistently through the daunting underworld combat so mutationally entailed, but now as genitally well harnessed in an increasingly cognizant manner, to elevationally reach by such dualistic amative means a novel insemination of finer awakening intelligence in the greening love-garden of the archetypal fathomful Heart thereby lushly caringly fertilized and wealthfully consequently flourishing, to finally result, narratively, in the sterling natal blossoming of an emergent ego integrity of strengthening substantive proportions simultaneously becoming aware and accepting of its vivistic homosexual nature, confirmed terminologically through the crowning grounded assumption of a transcendentally-valued gay identity.

In this verdurous Way of the good homosexual Heart, as a legitimate alternative mode of beneficially differentiating the feeling function to a heterosexual approach for the estimable sake of achieving a sure sensibility of singularly meaningful personhood constitutionally well-actualized, a prospectively-oriented gay man is more than adequately empowered symbolically to finally complete the escalating rungs of the luminatory Divine Ladder and celebratorily enter that heavenly abiding relationship with his beautifully perfected twin-soul which they have both so passionately desired, the noble quest rewardingly well fulfilled at this appropriate level of inward challenge and compositional growth, true gay love humanistically redeemed to a satisfyingly-embodied adult life, the deserving hero existentially exalted to that valued degree from developmental failure and life-crippling shame. This most loving embrace and richly productive bonding with the hot breath-buddy double-soul successfully channels and auspiciously transforms the upwelling crude libido of primal instinctual psyche to forge a viable bond with the archetypal Self vigorously sustaining a realistically sturdy sense of reliably stable ego in harmoniously well-rooted gay identity and dedicated to the assertive functioning of an enhancedly felt and clarifyingly known personhood that, in this salubriously-constituting way, valuationally includes the basic masculine and feminine qualities. Healthy gay identity formation, then, consists metaphorically of the ancient initiatory journey through the darkly chthonic realms shamanically by which a responsibly desirous man crowningly renewingly gains a treasured sense of more androgynous or whole self in a robust figurative partnership of inner beauteous strength and wonderfully inspiring creativity with the all-encompassing God of most meaningfully fulfilled and capaciously awakened personality as valuably homosexual.

Within the budding subjectivity of a fortunate gay-man-to-be, the vital double-soul is celestially fatefully aroused and amorously mesmerically calls out to him phallically, and if such a nobly designated boy heartfully enough responds to that numinous invitation to the epic narrative Romance which is mythically entailed in this fiery geminating signal, he thereupon lets the instigated wraith-buddy into his freshly-emergent life to now well sprout up involvingly thereso, and in due gestational course the fruitional struggle is actively then joined between striving proto-consciousness and the prospectively disputatious unconscious that we have been exploring. Successful psychic resolution is the solid establishment of a luminous "perfected soul" able to maturationally sustain the conflictual opposites within it and in fecund relation to it, a wholesome state well symbolized by auspiciously-accomplished twinship marriage figurations from historical myth such as the ultimate reunion of Horus-and-Seth and that of the Greek Dioscouri, the astrological Gemini. The dialectical bivalence of the soulfully aroused double archetype typically expresses itself metaphorically as light/dark, above/below, older/younger, immortal/

mortal, refined/coarse, dominant/submissive, even as male/female (Fabricius, 1976, p. 39). If the glorious Dew of glittering Heaven incarnationally appears, majestically inseminated by the godly archetypal Self as the well-earned product of its committed evolutional love, then the relationally hungry opposites are satisfyingly reconciled in full return and superior renewal at the liminal Source of individually experienced existence, and a newly distinguished, better integrated, and improvedly energized wholeness of humanely coherent personality will in due course be realizationally achieved therefrom. That refined subjective wholeness, in turn, amounts metaphorically to the wealthfully incorporating expression of magnanimous Aphrodite Urania well categorically actualized, who safely contains and reliably nurtures the tangibly living universe of worthy Uranian love within her thus-so substantiating "body" of increasingly-commodious felt experience of meaningful existential being as a same-sex-loving person.

This informative imagery is the considered result to our allegorical amplification of a possible gay soul-figure in early personality development, and describes the subjective evolutional workings of a procreative Uranian *coniunctio* or homosexual alchemical marriage symbolism in gay-centered analytic terms of its principal operating metaphors, an archetypally self-awakening conformation for self-determinationally growing good gay personhood that we can now thematically encapsulate as the riveting *Romance of the Phallic Double*, as the hypnotic *Haunting of the Wraith-Buddy Soul*. This omnivorously haunting Romance assuredly induces, and manifestly consists of, a dynamic invigorative sequence in the personally emergent psyche of thesis-antithesis-synthesis, through which prior libidinal combinations are dialectically broken down and freshly expansive wholes are transcendentally created in an ongoing mutational incorporation of healthful elemental development in viable psychological existence as gay, a refining differentiation and progressive reintegration of cumulative valuational effect amatively fueled atomically from an infinitely surging source by intelligent homosexual libido, by the spirit of heavenly Uranian Eros. Thus figuratively considered, the purposive Romance of the vital double-soul, once set into fateful teleological motion through the shaping Uranian complex, can be regarded as a greening "motor" of goodly subjective evolution in modern gay men, as well as producing a most-valuable end result, the tangible creation of treasurable new consciousness and emporeringly felt personhood, wholesome gay individuation of the fertile subjective domain proceeding through successive enactments of the incestuous Uranian *coniunctio* motif.

The twin-soul itself, as we can see in exploring the related ancient Egyptian idea of the *Ka*, can further be amplified as actually consisting of seven constituent pairs of complementary aspects thematically articulating a qualitatively-ascending nutritional sequence, from elementary "Subsistence" to "Splendour" and "Radiance" (Lamy, 1981, p. 26), with each "satisfied" pair forming an improvemental "step" on the resulting transportive "ladder" of its aggregate embodied maturation. This uplifting pattern, of course, is that metaphorical Divine Ladder of verdant valuational Perfection in the sacred psychic heartland of homosexual romantic love that we have already looked at in terms of the transcendent call to venereal mutuality between an enthusiastic man and his essential same-sex soul-figure, and from this comparative observation it can be considered that only with the fully actualized development of all fourteen qualitative soul-aspects can a devoted gay man victoriously ascend to the Ladder's completory top, just as the shining sunboat is successfully harnessed in Egyptian thought with Ra's seven pairs of renewed soul-twin qualities when it triumphantly conveys him beaming anew into the virgin sky at dawn. We might well imagine, then, that in sen-

sibly considering the likely shape of wholesome gay individuation to its entire psychological completion, we could analogously see the aggregate buddy-soul itself materializationally
develop with the ego along a larger Uranian Ladder through
seven distinct forms, seven shining epiphanies of the origina-
tory inspiriting Essence, each brightly constituted form even
more richly refined compositionally than the one before it,
each relationally integrating with the partnering man in an
again-enlarged identity and personality to progressively "pull"
him up to confront the growthful Typhonian sequence of a
new double-form at the next expansive level of possible aggregate individuation.

From this broadened perspective, the contemporary
formation of laudable gay identity can be depthfully pictured as reflecting one full "working" of the motoric Divine
Ladder's mutational effectuation realizationally in the subjective Eternal Heart of fervent gay desire, as a purposeful
motivating force for just-so specifyingly growing valued
psychic incorporation homosexually. So we can appropriately imagine that when a sincere gay man is able to productively bond with his genitally conjugated double in a
sustaining ego-Self axis, or connection to the archetypal
Self, through a well-empowered and fluently-nurturant gay
identity reliably secured ideologically, he has achieved the
first elevating rung, liberatorily, on a more-comprehensive
Divine Ladder of his wealthful elemental potential for full
subjective particularization, for example to take a Hindu
metaphor, the kundalini energy has been seminally aroused
in the bottom, Muladhara chakra of a bigger possible
wholeness, eloquently manifesting the centralizing ego-Self
axis there in the firm "earth" of a good self-concept as
worthily integrally gay. This solid constitutional success
would in metaphorical turn represent the least conscious,
least individuated level of satisfyingly confirmed relation-

ship elementally possible realizationally with the vivifying double as soul, but also as capably containing the still more estimable potential for six additional forms of increasing constituent "perfection" within itself, each in generational succession procreatively rising from the prior one through greater conscious self-realization, and productively cultivated cumulatively until all the fulfilled fundamental qualities of the thereby overarchingly-perfected soul are well valuationally collected. Such a larger appreciation can accordingly motivate in the now-integrated gay ego identity a more-advanced transformational undertaking to more purposefully work with one's own personal psychology within this much-extended mythic context, first, that endeavor actively entailed in fairly facing one's psychic shadow-side of complicated feelings and private themes, through which a more-fathomful layer of transpersonal symbolic involvement can be better gradually apprehended and partnered, particularly with the aid of relevant facilitative methods, such as Jungian dreamwork, amplification, and active imagination, about which I will have more to say in subsequent talks.

Sure logistical efforts to enter this wealthfully more-verdant portal of superior gay becoming will likely lead symbolically to better enlightening participation in that incestuous sacred union *mysterium* which, in the imaginal comprehension we are here following out, is of the largest prospective importance to meaningfully gestating subjectivity homosexually, an archetypally-sourced *Hieros Gamos* or Sacred Marriage with the soul-brother double that wondrously and obscenely recreates in same-sex-loving form the creational font of the originating Primal Scene, whose joyous wedding ceremony reversingly ends fatefully in that bleak mortality initiatorily leading necessarily into the foreboding but fruitful underworld now opened up accessibly through painful feeling life thoroughly related to, expressed, and processed. The ultimate product of such a heartfelt sacrificial undertaking will felicitously be the shining golden disc of gloriously revealing Wisdom, the all-endowing elixir of magnificently refined Life, the rejuvenated, wish-granting phoenix of royally transcendent Treasure, indeed, all those evocative experiential and mystical metaphors referencing the richest valuational goal sincerely aimed for passionately by the finally-ineffable alchemical Art of sagaciously expediting energetically-enriching Self-realization profitably at last tangibly most well achieved qualitatively in upfront homosexual form.

In sum, because we can today consider realistically reaching toward such a gay-centered Jungian comprehension about the ultimate homosexual individuation of improvedly valuable personality, as we have just here done, it can well be appreciated historically that, while on the more-shady side there are current limitations in standard gay liberation ideologies of serious note, there have also been quite-successful beneficial effects in helping provide confirmed lesbian and gay peoples the outstanding chance to now purposefully enter the numinous doorway of cultivated psychological awareness more carefully.

In addition to the ideas and establishment of the Institute for Contemporary Uranian Psychoanalysis that I have just touched on, we can also see the critically-waking urge to become improvedly psychological expressed today in the L.A. gay community by the parallel founding of the local Antioch University's LGBT graduate psychotherapy specialization and that of psychologist Don Kilhefner's Gay Men's Medicine Circle, which also purports to have a homosexual psychological interest and understanding. All these pioneering efforts are to be warmly applauded, yet it should be noted that Antioch's academic program is limited in its intellectual depth and research capabilities, while Dr. Kilhefner's otherwise-progressive discussions of gay psychology, as for example entailed in his various magazine articles calling for gay "adults" and "elders," for a homosexual "soul-led" rather than "ego-driven" life, and so on, are unfortunately tainted by a persistent trivialization of gay subjective actualities that corrupts and compromises legitimate psychological concepts and methods, a problem to which I will return in greater detail in the following talk.

From these overall-mixed conditions as to the serious study, understanding, and promotion of gay-centered psychological liberation, we can appreciate how fresh, challenging, and powerful this innovative step toward better-enhanced homosexual emancipation must surely be, one requiring as much disciplined attention, specialized thoughtfulness, sensitive responsibility, and sustained implementation as possible. Thus, inauguration of the Institute for Contemporary Uranian Psychoanalysis.

I would also at this point like to note, in outlining what I believe is our moral activist duty as progressive homosexual people to historically take up a gay-centered psychology, that I feel this epic responsibility most strongly in regard to the younger generations of same-sex-loving folk just coming up now, who will only increasingly be inheriting the challenging contemporaneous factors which I detailed earlier in this discussion. As time inevitably marches on, the need for a viable alternative to old-fashioned homophobic bigotry, on the one hand, and current gay assimilationism, on the other, as an effective sustaining spark to our Gay Liberation Movement's finest fulfilled future, will only grow more insistent, and it is the young, in the end, who will be best positioned to take fullest advantage of the unprecedentedly wonderful but supremely challenging opportunity now shaping up socioculturally to reach for improvedly-estimable homosexual realization personally.

Will we gay folk now effectively enough take up this golden historic crossroads chance opportunely being hingingly proffered, to more intently follow Aphrodite Urania and her beguiling Eros illuminationally into the finer healing and wondermental initiations of estimable shamanic becoming that are most gainfully made operatively available psychologically? Are we ready to treat homosexual love and identity as a lifelong gnostic calling to questingly attain the farther reaches of individual symphonic wholeness and unique bejeweling enhancement in body, mind, and soul by which a new kind of interpersonal world can be better effectively expedited into realistic birth, a new political, social, economic, and familial world of universal subjective justice, liberation, and empowerment, a long needed, successfully caring world of moral human beings and the true beginning of legitimately human history rather than the proto-human, prehistoric era of forgetful psychological irresponsibility currently still fraudulently gripping our society self-righteously today, the viciously primitive "law of the jungle" of unexamined ego defenses and resistant interpersonal collusions?

We same-sex-loving peoples have often served in forward-seeing capacities in many different cultures and times, but it seems to me that none has been moreso ethically important than what is here and now provocatively being opened up to us so advantageously by the timely growth of serious gay-centered psychology. I invite you to join with me in this crucial activist project for more directly advancing humanistic homosexual actualization introvertedly and collectively as it unfolds productively in the coming months and years, and thereby participate auspiciously through procreative regeneration of Gay Liberation salubriously in the satisfactional incarnation of wealthfully-enlarged fay meaningfulness on a fructiferous scale and with a foundational scope possibly limited only by the imagination and efforts of the practitioner, the marvelous protean chance to homosexually contributorily redeem the larger failings and missed opportunities of the sorrowfully benighted past for the stellar aeonic sake of a necessarily more-equitable era to come if humanity is to at-all adequately survive its present developmental crisis. Thank you.

PHILOSOPHORVM.

Gay Liberation at a Psychological Crossroads: The New Ethical Importance of Psychological Responsibility in Furthering the Next Stage of Homosexual Emancipation and in Founding the ICUP

In terms of historical time, the most important civilizational story of our current era, in my opinion, is and has been for a considerable period one about the humanization of subjectivity, by which I mean the realizational growth of valuable personhood. This broad humanistic development of individual authority has been evolving over the past several centuries in a deepening struggle with the prior morality of selfhood as defined and controlled by forces and sources external to it, and to this point the new valuation has succeeded sufficiently that its basic rubric is now enshrined in the constitutions and laws of most nations and the United Nations under such ideas as "human rights," "human dignity," and so on, although the historic contention between these clashing traditions continues unabated throughout the world today.

I would like to suggest that much of the impetus for and perpetuation of this innovative historical direction has been due to those people wishing to freely explore the meaning and experience of what we might call an alternative sexual lifestyle while under extendedly intolerant conditions. And when that vernal ethical direction had progressed significantly in influential effect, yet still had not liberalized the general social tolerance adequately enough to allow for what today would be described as an "out gay person," the particular conditions were gestationally ready for the grassroots birth of a specifically Homosexual Liberation Movement, which in consequence has been a substantial presence among humanity now for about the past 150 years.

During that notable time, we homosexuals have gradually evolved a name and an identity for ourselves that nurture and inform the humanization of being a same-sex-loving person of dignity, value, and contributive creative potential. We have, by way of many generations, gone through a long journey of gradual self-awakening and discovery, from initial musings about who we were, to a variety of alternate understandings and terminologies, to today's proud and self-respecting lesbian- and gay-identified peoples. The power, importance, and influence of this cumulative authorizational achievement can hardly be underestimated, as it dramatically demonstrates the new ethic of personal authenticity and self-determination reciprocally operating within a supportive collective context. Thus, to be securely homosexually-identified today is to be a walking beacon of inspiration for everybody to better awaken the spirit of independent truth within, a truly radical spirit in the political sense, a signal redistributive spirit which, if it were to finally accomplish its actualizational aims successfully enough, it seems to me, would see the conclusive extirpation of human societies and so-called "civilizations" that, no matter how seemingly sophisticated and tolerant, are actually still steeped in barbaric brutality and violent exploitation, both physical and mental.

Because homosexuality has been and is ongoingly today so fiercely attacked and scapegoated, it enacts a brave heroism to integrate a solid gay identity, one that amounts, symbolically, to a classic initiatory death and rebirth experience. As, for example, perhaps most notably described academically by Vivienne Cass's six-stage model of homosexual identity formation (Cass, 1979), one falls into an untethered state of painful confusion about the orientational intent and meaning of one's genital development at a certain influential point as one grows up being socialized in a homophobic, heterotriumphalist culture, thereby entering on a self-questioning "dark night of the soul," as the Jungians might say, to eventually reach a reformational reconstitution of essential self-comprehension at a better-integrated level of fruitful gay being and functioning. In this decisive way is activated an internal alchemy of elemental transformational improvement, and one moves categorically from condemnatorily feeling like a darkling outcast from the succoring company of the Divine Spark of all meaning and significance, to the redeeming dawn of a greater and more true tie felt between oneself and that transcendent valuation within, a regenerated bond assuredly knotted in a salutarily-clarified homosexual identity.

Thus so do modern gay people enact an age-old shamanic heritage, by becoming and being soundly identifiedly gay. But I would argue that that necessary transformative journey is not altogether finished to a sufficient extent with the securing of a good homosexual identification, which is rather like the first large step on a longer path to requisitely more-complete self-fulfillment. We who are same-sex loving live in an overarching societal world that pretty much continues to ignore and denigrate us terribly, and, in my opinion, the best of various worthy ways to actively combat the nefarious influence which a cruelly-bigoted system ongoingly exerts against our self-esteem and integrity, is to keep growing and deepening oneself as a homosexual person in association with like-minded others in the most direct manner possible. Further, just as insidious as the venomous impact of current social bias on maintaining and expanding gay self-vibrancy, is the difficult fact that all of us have probably grown up in families that were ideologically based in anti-homosexual attitudes buttressed by an entire social world so odiously polluted, and we have likely absorbed much intellectual and emotional poison therefrom that can badly thwart good self-care and maturational progress throughout life, especially as such internal problems resonate with ongoing sociocultural prejudice while one is in the legitimate pursuit of worthy adult goals such as stable intimate love and worthwhile creative achievement.

This watershed problem of the incompleted journey to become fully liberatedly gay within oneself after identificationally "coming out," was individually described exemplificationally in last Fall's issue of *The Gay & Lesbian Review Worldwide* (2008), in the reprinted remarks by gay scholar Martin Duberman upon receiving the Harvard Gay and Lesbian Caucus's "Founding Father Award" last June ("Taking the 'Cure' at Harvard in the 50's"). This is what he said:

> You see, for me gay liberation has always been something of a misnomer. Once you accept yourself and join a community, that isn't the equivalent of immediately establishing self-acceptance. I think it's an initial strategy whereby the process has a chance to begin. But by signing up for—wherever you place yourself in time—the Mattachine Society or ACT UP, that doesn't bring with it anything like self-acceptance overnight....For me, the process, even in my advanced years, remains ongoing. Liberation is something that I'm certain will never be complete. On a daily basis I still have to grapple with a lot of what was done to me more than fifty years ago. I have to grapple with the scars, the deep, permanent scars that remain....(p. 29)

Thus we arrive at the more-developed notion of a *second stage* or phase of gay identity formation after its solid establishment, in which that clarified identity now redemptively comes to better terms with its psychological underpinnings in the ongoing pursuit of enhanced personal fulfillment as successfully homosexual. Places inside that are still wounded, thwarted, distorted, and so on by formative or present experiences of bigotry and other malignant forces must be effectively identified and reparatively addressed to further secure, empower, enrich, and extend the meaning and value of estimable homosexual personhood, not only to rescue ourselves determinationally from malevolent social victimization, but even more importantly, to thereby advance the beauty and brightness of being valuably same-sex loving as an encouraging beacon of hope for the eventual achievement of human self-realization overall.

Therefore, a second stage in gay identity formation concerns the efficacious development of *psychological awareness*, the capacity to see and engage the interiorly-known world of experienced images and feelings in progressive terms of the salient developmental issues suchwise being presented for that gay person, particularly those issues implicating how the cognizant self—the "ego"—*feels* about itself. To support this novel functional direction and circumstantiate the resulting comprehension to be attained homosexually in committedly following out its better actualization, is the productive purpose of ideologically distinguishing a useable *gay psychology*, and indeed is the propulsive reason for the existence of the Institute for Contemporary Uranian Psychoanalysis altogether.

Certainly, because same-sex-loving peoples insistently do and will continue to show an abiding interest in existing and consolidating themselves as such, and because doing so embodies such a powerfully-progressive impulse of broad social and political relevance, the necessity to helpfully grasp homosexual personality development and lifetime functioning, in a wide range of pertinent contexts, will only suitably grow. And while there are established associations of LGBT psychiatrists, psychologists, therapists, etc., and the publication of various books in this topical area, even graduate training programs in "gay-affirmative" psychology, there has never been a scholarly and professional center until now rigorously dedicated to homosexual psychological functioning and wholesome individuation, a serious research and training facility for more effectually advancing the better theoretical and practical comprehension of what aptly could be called "gay-centered psychology," by which I mean a respectful attempt to systematically apprehend and usefully facilitate same-sex-loving subjectivity healthfully.

The current times require pioneering such an introvert formulational direction due to the pressing need for better psychological awakening in society generally and in gay and lesbian people particularly. By "better psychological awakening" I mean that which results from a more conscious encounter with oneself as a *psychological being*, as an entity consisting of existential subjectivity in its immediacy, that is, the mental functioning and experience of psychic life, the world of private thoughts, images, feelings, sensations, associations, themes, layers, and mysteries, in relation to itself, as it is or can be aware of itself, feeling itself, and so on. I say "as it can be" experienced in addition to how it is presently doing so, to suggest a non-static quality and growthful potentiality to self-awakening psychological existence that allow for the most interesting manifestational possibilities.

My concern here is with the development of humanity as a *psychological species*. From this point of view, physical life has emerged from the mud on earth through evolving the spinal cord and then the brain in order to bring about the presence and evolution of electrically-based subjective life, finally culminating in that non-material existence successfully becoming conscious of and in itself. It is with the challenge of this latter step that humanity finds itself struggling mightily today. Rather than gracefully embracing such a momentous historical opportunity, of course, most people seem quite oblivious to the remarkable opening auspiciously being epochally offered, if they are not downright hostile to its improved realistic recognition. Yet the accumulating evolutionary pressure to accountably take up the veritable fact of being psychological only increases reciprocally as it is denied irresponsibly, and this stalemating dilemma has led inevitably to the strange waste and distracted stagnation presently characterizing such extravertedly-biased, post-industrial societies as the United States of America.

An earlier age might have described this kind of deep-rooted social malaise in traditional religious terms, or perhaps philosophically, just as current exteriorizing attitudes might locate it sociologically, economically, or in history, if it is even recognized at all. But ever since Sigmund Freud began to systematically notice how people seemed so much to be privately motivated consistently by irrational unconscious forces of usually unfortunate consequence, it is in my estimation more relevant to frame the matters under our consideration here as "psychological" in the sense that Freud and his ideological successors have been broadly concerned with, the world of human subjectivity seen in terms of psychodynamic relations.

This intellectual perspective, within which I would include formulational offshoots such as humanistic and cognitive-behavioral approaches, has arisen and persisted because of humanity's surging need for a better-specifying theory and practice of evolutionary mental enhancement than offered by previous or presently-competing traditions, one that is first of all more effectively able to identify and address the existential problem of psychological responsibility in the context of personal authenticity, that is, the ethical necessity entailed in sincere individual becoming to properly take ownership more consciously of one's own "psychological business," one's inner emotional and functional issues, rather than be otherwise unconsciously dominated by them through psychological defensive mechanisms such as projection, dissociation, acting out, collusion, and so on, automatic mechanisms that lawlessly enable and misbegottenly perpetuate horrific forms of symbolic and literal, individual and collective, violence, such as child abuse, murder, group scapegoating, and totalitarianism. It is this most-intimate relationship between a person and her or his own personal psychology, it seems to me, that is at the historic crux of humanity's fate and freedom today, in that liberatory self-realization inevitably leads to facing internally oppressive forces manifested in one's charged self-relations, so as to rightfully reach a rejuvenated degree of authentic self-actualizational empowerment, legitimate existential becoming, and ultimate valuational fulfillment unprecedented in finally reparatively addressing humanity's perpetually destructive infantilism.

Indeed, it seems to me that through the better pursuit of personal psychological responsibility, a psychoanalytic worldview provides for a second crucial arena of more-accurate theory and practice in the aeonic shift of fundamental values now historically underway, one of perhaps even greater importance than that of subjective ownership itself, one concerned with the pursuit of ultimate spiritual matters and essential transcendental meanings. This thematic direction has become the particular provenance of Jungian analytic formulations, because, whereas Freud held to the more traditional "scientific" view that individual humanization meant the "secularization" of human nature, Jung increasingly came to appreciate the great possibility in reformulationally transitioning human spirituality into the individual not only as "the dignity of man," but as well the font of all legitimate spiritual experience and revelation autonomously sourced in regard to the ego-personality undergoing it. Thus, in Jungian thought, what before was obscuringly imagined to be objectively "out there" fabulously, as heaven and hell, angels and devils, is now more realistically reimagined, in a carefully analytically parsed-out way, as subjectively "within," still of transcendental constitution but, as such, materially existing inside an animated private terrain as vast as the one without that includes all which has been discovered by Freudian-oriented psychoanalysis, the method Jung held to most seriously and effectively engage the *retrospective* psyche, those aspects of personal being shaped by prior experiences, and through which one could gain better access to the *prospective* psyche, that aspect involved with *future* possibilities, especially those of what Jung often called "numinous" importance, meaning, supernatural and sacred. Thus is it so that, as individual loyalty of being conclusively leaves the group loyalty of outside definition, it can advantageously redeem the severe loss of always-reliable collective inflation fatefully entailed in that epic orientational shift through constructive self-realization of its own teleological nature in a restorative interiorization of ultimate spiritual reality, practice, and realization, a most fundamental authorizational transferral from the synagogue/church/mosque/etc., the rabbi/priest/imam/etc., the literal heaven and earth, to the individually-discrete personal heart, not only the divine become human in this lovely relocational fashion, but the human justly become revaluationally divine as well. This is what Jung meant by completory psychological individuation.

Here is that powermental, methodological bridge between the primordial era of human group-mindedness and the more grown-up phase of individual justice, extended most importantly into the realm of spiritual desire and meaning, an ideological step of the greatest expeditive possibility, because nothing motivates human nature that is not, at heart, legitimately and autonomously felt as "divine," it seems to me, and nothing charges up people as much as that incitement conveying the magic of transcendent valuations. Thus, because the evolution of human-transpersonal intimacy will lead to the final redemption of "God" as much as that of imperfectly-unconscious human beings, the strongest authority and spiritual potentiality is likewise then correspondingly conveyed significationally to and in the realizational act of wholesome personal individuation, according to Jungian analytic psychology.

Now, consider this Jungian humanizational understanding in regard to freely and fairly becoming gay-identified in the shamanic alchemical sense we considered before, as a legitimate individuational enactment, and one can see in the resulting amplification new symbolic dimensions to such basic phenomena as homosexual desire, romance, orientation, identity, history, liberty, community, and self-chosen terminology of profoundly expanded scope and import, for example in terms of the favorable historical evolution of a more individually differentiated ego-Self axis or consciously personalized experience of psychic Providence. Not only does such an affirmative Jungian appreciation strategically extend the sense in being same-sex loving as a "natural" or spontaneous self-particularization legitimizationally into the specific conceptual and applied domains so powerfully explored in the Jungian tradition, as I touched on at greater length in my previous talk, but it does so practically as well in terms of better-distilled relationship to that symbolic Homosexual Divinity which is pictured evocatively as the mythic shining progenitor of gay sex, love, identity, and finer maturational futurity.

In my opinion, this is where it starts to truly get more interesting as to the pertinence and worth of developing a gay-centered psychological attitude, meaning a compassionate analytical approach that takes up the viewpoint of subjective gay phenomena themselves: Moreso useful even than addressing the problems of internalized homophobia and traumatized experience for their own reparative sake, is to justly do so in more progressive order to then be better personally empowered and enabled to develop those transpersonal qualities and possibilities in being valuably homosexual that I have only alluded to so far in passing tonight, as I have mainly tried to stay with the basic notion of homosexual subjective oppression and freedom, and the necessary development of gay psychological responsibility for difficult personal issues in order to effectively gain greater inner liberation.

But it is the case, in my experience, that as one increasingly attains sufficient psychological competence with one's personally-troublesome shadow dynamics, one is further transformed into an adequate partner to all those other aspects and layers of one's experience that invoke and involve transpersonal values and forces, such that, in consequence, additionally-advanced possibilities of good self-realization become practically attainable involving those greater forces that previously the personality was too weak or immature to adequately handle or even consider. And as such constructive relationship with the transpersonal is cultivated in the activist context of this growing psychological mindedness, it in turn contributes to the improved functioning of subjective self-responsibility, because the value of inwardly caring for oneself better is effectuationally enhanced by stronger contact with the inestimably transcendent when that can be sufficiently personally handled.

Even though powers beyond the normal or human are always around us and in us, in my opinion, it is another matter entirely to face such powers more directly or purposefully within, where the worth of one's own meaning and integrity will be accordingly provoked. Without a solid and ongoing practice of partnering and dealing with one's shadow-side psychologically, in my experience, there cannot be a more practical advancement into better engaging the transpersonal responsibly, that is, without fatal contamination by personally-violent unconscious motives.

On the other hand, with the problem of the shadow appropriately identified and accounted for, it also becomes apparent that a fully-ethical psychological responsibility ultimately includes recognition and cultivation of one's personal relations to subjective homosexual numinosity as much as to regressive shadow business as such. Indeed, the shadow itself is numinous, in its power, its opposition, its ability to confound, although it may be hard to appreciate these larger features when one is badly in their grip! Accordingly, then, along with coming to terms with one's private issues concerning the conflictual past, there should also be included a more straightforward approach to appreciating how and where the experience of the transcendent is manifesting in regard to the evolutionary future, not only in the encounter with the shadow specifically, but in the more-pertinent overall context of being gay and growing better as a homosexually-maturing psychological and emotional person.

I am saying that being gay itself is highly numinous, first of all, in the magic and power of same-sex love, not only as romantic sexual love but as homosexual, as involving someone genitally like oneself, a double double magic strengthened even better by its relative rarity in the larger society, thus accounting for some of those rather prominent features that could unfortunately most attract the general problem of social scapegoating. But there is more. In loving a person of the same sex, one will feel a stronger commonality with heterosexual people of the opposite sex than with those of similar sex, thus highlighting a much more androgynous relationship to gender than is the parallel case in heterosexual psychology. This androgyny, along with that familiarity to the love-object in same-sex bonding which also contrasts so strongly with heterosexual symbolic relations, both contribute to that transcendent capability in being gay described in many world cultures of being a bridge between the worlds, say in shamanism, or between the heterosexual genders, as many Native American and other berdache figures were said to serve. I would even go further, and suggest that these androgynous and same-sex-loving features are also very germane to interior self-relations, subjectively speaking, that they position the person so endowed to better learn to listen and relate with oneself inside, thus contributing to the evolutionary cultural birth not only of shamanism but later of more sophisticated spiritual systems, religion, philosophy, science, and psychoanalysis. And on top of that, if we then consider these homosexual features as being selected by the self-differentiating, archetypal Self to be the subjective ground for a focally-identifying personal ego experience, the sense of a self-awakening homosexual individuality, of gay personhood, particularly during this budding post-Enlightenment era still beginning historically of individual enfranchisement which I have been discussing tonight—with all this profound, compounding signification, then it becomes easily imaginable as to how, where, and why being gay today might be numinous, and most importfully so! Learning to assume appropriate responsibility for such a rich endowment, then, would surely indicate a markedly significant recovery by a caring, same-sex-loving person from toxic homophobic poisoning.

This is where the Jungian contribution to psychoanalytic thought I touched on before can be very useful to a gay-centered psychology, in better drawing out the sense of transpersonal homosexual individuation suggested by this talk. Indeed, because of the tremendously-appealing significance of the profoundly-synthesized ideological direction progressively offered to more-advanced political ideologies of sub-jective liberation in particular by Jungian analytic methodol-ogy, it can well be appreciated that, if the overall historical project of psychoanalysis, broadly considered, is finally suffi-ciently efficacious, then its organizational advent marks ini-tiatory passage to a legendarily novel, psychologically-focused age of universally-enhanced human growth and functioning for everyone of an entirely-unprecedented scope and fertility.

The difficulty of working effectively enough to realisti-cally approach such a bounteous global reformation, however, can scarcely be soberly underestimated when we commonly see people around us, gay and straight, and indeed whole societies, continue avoiding adequate responsibility for those crucial and difficult psychological issues which are so venomously existent in everyone's subjectivity. As we then consider that, for those who are homosexual, there is the added challenge of historic and current homophobia, a ter-rible social evil most often rampantly present starting within a lesbian or gay child's own family of origin, and aiming to cruelly thwart the wonderful individuational possibilities in being homosexual I outlined in a suggestive way just before now, it can well be appreciated how significant it would be for same-sex-loving people to cultivate a proficient language of serious self-reflection that introversionally enables and facilitatively enacts becoming better psychologically minded as valuably homosexual.

And, as I will again reiterate, such an interior relational language is so very much needed not just to overcome the awful effects of societal ugliness past and present, but better yet to multiplicationally strengthen being salutarily gay by cultivating the further procreative possibilities of that auspi-cious self-alchemy inaugurated by the historic subjective accomplishment of forging a caring gay self-acceptance. Indeed, when we appreciate that homosexual interest may have been a strong factor all along in the rise of subjective liberation altogether, thus of the psychoanalytic movement in particular as one of its foremost products and tools, then the more-overt extension of gay liberation thinking into psychoanalytic comprehension now being required of us, may not then seem like merely an ideologically otherwise-haphazard marriage, more like a post-heterosexist reunion, especially if we then consider the likely presence of considerable homosexual impulses in important psychoanalytic founders such as Freud and Jung, not to mention additional related phenomena such as Jung becoming surrounded by a number of strong women followers called his "Valkyries," most of whom were lesbian.

But the viciousness of homophobia, I think, has previously thwarted a better exploration of valuable gay being through apposite psychoanalytic terms in regard to the functional development by homosexual people of an accelerated psychological attitude. Today's more pressing circumstances, however, are working an emancipatory change in this unproductive status quo. That redemptive spirit behind the realization of a good gay identity has, in my opinion, unleashed an autonomously-sourced, alchemical transformative process not altogether satisfied by rightfully gaining a solid homosexual identification, and the expanding success of gay liberation efforts in our own time, then, only primes that more forward-seeking interest additionally. Moreover, so as to not eventually fall back, progressively-speaking, from our current valuational accomplishments in the face of ongoing corrosive homophobia toxically combined with defensive complacency over our just gains along with the soothing reductionism of those assimilationist ideologies that have for some time dominated the same-sex-loving community, and instead to proceed into the greater emancipatory future promissorily held out today by the historically-ongoing Gay Liberation

Movement, then we must attempt a next stage in gay liberation theory and practice that includes and complements our
prior extravert gains, a more-introverted stage much more
thoroughly focused on enlarged psychological freedom,
ultimate individuational fulfillment, and the properly-
corresponding collective conditions best expediting such
personal gay enhancement. This is the fundamental challenge
now facing self-confirmed homosexuals, in my opinion: to
attemptedly produce through this farsighted, enabling means
the richest gay alternative to heterosexual biological procreation viably achievable today, as the most favorable way to
refoundationally revitalize our community, our Movement,
and our contribution to the world.

It is for the purpose of addressing this most critical developmental possibility in homosexual psychological engender-
ment that the Institute for Contemporary Uranian
Psychoanalysis has been founded. I and others of the Institute
indeed feel that cultivating a gay-centered psychological language, and facilitating a better-refined psychological attitude
among gay people, are of principal empowermental and
redemptive importance at this pregnant time. I am sure many
other same-sex-loving folk are also feeling this fulcrumatic
directional import, yet the organized response by our community as illustrated here in the Los Angeles area has so far
been rather mixed. Besides noting those ongoing professional
situations such as Antioch University's LGBT specialization,
the Gay and Lesbian Center's Mental Health Services
Department, and the Lesbian and Gay Psychotherapy Association of Southern California, all of which may be addressing
improved homosexual psychological awakening up to some
modest point, the only significant direct response I have seen
so far hereabouts in addition to the Institute for Contemporary Uranian Psychoanalysis and its sister affiliate, the Center
for Sapphic Psychoanalytic Studies founded by the late Sandra

Golvin, is that effort being mounted by psychologist Don Kilhefner and his Gay Men's Medicine Circle, which ostensibly also concerns a gay-centered Jungian approach to homosexual psyche, soul, and better valuational fulfillment.

However, that approach, at least as so far described in various print and web sources, while it is the only other organized attempt I am aware of anywhere, besides that of the ICUP, to cultivate a sustained same-sex-oriented psychological attitude, that approach can at the same time be seen to be, when sensibly looked at more closely, as we will do in a moment, unfortunately psychologically shallow and homosexually trivializing, in what actually strikes me as a manipulative fashion that contradictorily discourages realistic psychological mindedness, thus so illustrating how grasping human psychology more directly is still tremendously challenging, and consequently why there needs to be a much more systematically-cultivated same-sex-loving response to the momentous invitational call being sent out urgently by epochal historical forces for a new stage of gay liberation theory and practice, one based on and dedicated to the sincere cultivation of homosexual psychological awareness and authenticity in a virgin political sense, one that, in its creditable honoring of ultimately-spiritual homosexual valuation, is consequently truly modeled in the new ethical paradigm of fulfilled subjective liberation, not in an attempted simulation of that new ethos as yet another defensive way to hopefully cover up a private entrapment in the old morality of the tired past, the abusive morality of pain, humiliation, and disinheritance.

Dr. Kilhefner and the Gay Men's Medicine Circle are to be applauded for raising community concern in broaching a same-sex-loving psychological perspective at all, yet their published pronouncements have persistently externalized the issues and signification of psychological phenomena, usually in the complete absence of directly articulating any actual interior landscape of gay psychodynamic functioning and change. For example, in one of his more notable statements of the past few years, "Gay Adults! Gay Adults! Where are you? Trusting the River of Life" (*White Crane*, Summer 2006), Dr. Kilhefner urged the improved homosexual development of that maturational status, which he explicitly noted to be archetypally informed in the Jungian sense, yet then the substance of such a gay "adult" was detailed only as "fulfill[ing]... important roles in the gay village." Absolutely nothing was said in this entire article about what I would consider to most significantly constitute *psychologically* becoming a gay adult, which concerns the sufficient maturation of responsible interior autonomy as a gay-identified person through the extended confrontation and self-alchemy of ego-shadow relations differentiationally within that can successfully lead homosexually to those increasingly spiritualized degrees of subjective qualitative presence, coherence, empowerment, insight, and wisdom psychodynamically described by Jungian analyst Edward Edinger in his classic book, *Ego and Archetype* (1972), as treasured products of the spinal ego-Self axis, which structurally ties us to the divine inside, revelatorily ascending into more conscious view.

This problem in Dr. Kilhefner's statements has gone on for years. Even when he probed into inner self-relations, matters were still exteriorized in an absolute fashion. For example, in the article "Night Movies. Pay Attention to Your Dreams...They Are Leading You Somewhere" (*White Crane*, Spring 2007, pp. 29-30), Dr. Kilhefner reported on two of his own dreams and how he handled them, in the first of which he was driving and saw up ahead a police roadblock, and then that very day he was really driving and there actually was a roadblock ahead that he was then easily able to elude, as he had outstanding warrants for his arrest, and therefore he'd had "a precognitive dream…that prepares us, a head's up, for what is to come," while in the second dream he was looking through "the Book of Knowledge" when his finger could not move from the entry for "dreams," this being an example of a "teleological" dream about "what your purpose is for being in this incarnation," which for him meant working with other people's dreams (as well as his own) as a "licensed Jungian psychologist" (p. 30).

However, there is nothing remotely Jungian about Dr. Kilhefner's handling of his dreams as recounted in this article, it appears to me, nor is there anything about his own internal dynamics at all, or about anything actually psychological even. The treatment of these dreams is in point of fact really pre-psychological and literalistic, an unfortunate regressive characteristic also shown by other followers of this approach, such as Dr. Kilhefner's associate, Roberto Blain, in his articles for the L.A. gay magazine *Frontiers*, for example, "Follow Your Yellow Brick Road," April 8, 2008, pp. 52, 54, on how he has handled his life in terms of his dreams and synchronicities.

Indeed, this demeaning trivialization of gay psychology while overtly seeming to promote its espousal, has continued persistently by Gay Men's Medicine Circle-type spokespeople. Then this past June, that distorted approach was finally publically and vociferously criticized in-depth by several Institute colleagues of mine at the annual conference of the Lesbian and Gay Psychotherapy Association of Southern California. And fairly soon after that, as if in response, appeared a uniquely different *Frontiers* piece by Dr. Kilhefner on September 9, 2008, p. 60, that novelly proclaimed, "Gay Men and the Great Father-Son Wound: The Inner Work," in which interior psychodynamic and archetypal topics were broached for the first and so far only more-extended time, and Dr. Kilhefner even refers to his "deep inner work to heal" his own

"Father-Son Wound," from which effort he founded a "Father Hunger" workshop 12 years ago.

However, in seeming response to criticized shortcomings, this fresh characterization of dark and difficult psychic matters for homosexual men still betrays a shallow and facile quality, in merely skimming over the seriousness and struggle of engaging the negative, in biasing attractive qualities over mysterious "unacceptable" qualities, in suggesting that taking his Father Hunger workshop will relatively easily and quickly solve deep psychological problems, in insinuating that he has so superiorily healed his own Great Father-Son Wound that he can now upbraid the general readers of his article, in high moral contrast, as unhealed cowards who can't wait to forget about what he's saying and "hurry back to…The Abbey."

Furthermore, there is nothing straightforward in Dr. Kilhefner's piece about the actual subjective substance of any of the challenging themes he mentions, only allusions. In particular, there is nothing about trauma, nothing about abuse, nothing about homophobia. Moreover, there is nothing about developing or deepening an ongoing partnership with the shadow-side; in fact, the word *shadow* is never mentioned. Additionally, there is nothing about any actual inner-work processes themselves; I suppose one has to take his workshop to find out anything practical. As well, there is nothing directly about emotion and the feeling capacity anywhere in the discussion except for the isolated mention of "disdain" and "awe." There is nothing at all about love and intimacy. On top of these deficits, there is nothing about being gay-centered, only common-sense recommendations that could be made to anybody in any group. Likewise, there is nothing about homosexually-centered archetypes, only generic theoretical motifs applied to gay situations. Moreso, there *is* a condescending and meanspirited denigration of gay men going on, such as in the critical comment, "I often see…gay men with bumper stickers on their cars that say: 'I Refuse to Grow Up!'" I have never seen such a bumper sticker myself, even once. Have you? At the same time, there is still an emphasis on the externalization of inner life and change as measured by a literalized "heroic task," which is patronizingly illustrated only in extravert and assimilationist terms, such as "completing three years in the Marines" and "opening one's own auto repair shop." Finally, there is an almost messianic, cure-all quality to the concluding anonymous listing of fabulously-redeemed prior participants as seeming proof of the workshop's, or Dr. Kilhefner's, apparently almost miraculous touch, personal authenticity, and conceptual accuracy.

And since this article on the "Great Father-Son Wound" appeared last September, his more-recent published writings, such as "The Gay Community in Crisis" in the Fall 2008 issue of the gay spirituality magazine *White Crane*, or his regular "Edging Out" column in *Frontiers*, have regressed back to the usual trivializing point of again barely mentioning anything actually psychological, or, indeed, not even that.

In other words, since all writers are reflected in their productions, Dr. Kilhefner is indicatively suggested by a critical sampling of his published pronouncements to perhaps be more so unconsciously acting out some inner conflictual issues through his attempted formulations than effectively and usefully perceiving homosexual psychological relations thereby, thus a sort of snake-oil salesman, and thus providing an instructive illustration of the very real dangers and formidable seriousness hazardously attendant to the otherwise noble and shining heroic quest for better gay psychological awareness. I might add mitigatingly, that in a general human world which is broadly fiercely biased against introvert legitimacy, many ostensibly well-trained psychologists and psychoanalysts of all sorts may actually have quite poorly-developed or -maintained psychological competence, again pointing out how original and challenging it is, in the human evolutionary sense, for anyone to seek better self-awareness within that personal realm which is oneself in the funhouse-mirrored halls of gripping psychological defenses, much less when the positive estimation of homosexuality, a form of love and personhood viciously and murderously condemned in Western Christian traditions for going on more than a thousand persistent years now, is at practical and realistic stake.

So, if we have just reviewed how not to best effectively cultivate better gay psychological awareness, then what might constitute the practicable opposite? Here we have the intent and nature of ongoingly developing what the Institute characterizes as "contemporary Uranian psychoanalysis," the first extended theory and practice to substantively address enhanced homosexual psychological self-awakening and maturational individuation as the necessary next stage of actual gay liberation, a trailblazing activist integration of homosexually centered valuation with Freudian- and Jungian-based psychoanalytic and other ideation that strikes me as a more really-adult type of caring concern for judiciously promoting and devotedly facilitating sincere "gay adulthood" and "gay elderhood" as internally-detailed shamanic states of alchemically more-advanced homosexual subjective becoming.

As to the emphatically-timely question of what more specifically does gay-affirmingly better build the introversional phenomenon I have been calling "psychological awareness" or being responsibly cognizant of one's "personal psychology" as a self-respecting, same-sex-loving person, I might point out that all my comments here today are sketching out aspects of what that more grown-up homosexual self-arousal might realistically entail, such as learning to progressively distinguish, relate to, and work with oneself interiorly in basic psychoanalytic, Jungian, and gay-appreciative terms, that is, to so comport oneself sincerely from inside one's subjectively encountered being itself as spontaneously manifested in privately known feelings, images, thoughts, etc., along with their thematically-dynamic object relations and symbolic import to each other and to the world outside subjectivity, for the valuative sake of satisfactionally reaching transcendent homosexual initiation. And for myself, I might add in all fairness and self-disclosure, this approach has meant many long years of supportively struggling to better face and engage my own developmentally-challenging "shadow business" of inner power relations, its corrupting inferiorities and better possibilities, my psychic defensive maneuvers, such as a trained sense of failure and inadequacy, traumatically perverted ambitions of rage-fueled revenge, and paralyzing hurt from vicious self-judgmentalness, vicissitudinous matters which I candidly seek to ongoingly partner, differentiate, and grow from as I experience my own felt life moment to moment homosexually and numinously.

But in addition to what I have so far pointed out about being gay-centered and psychologically minded, I would like to briefly add one more comment. From a classical Jungian point of view, meaning in terms of the system Jung and his immediate followers reached by the end of his life, everything which human beings do or can experience, create, or know is most essentially symbolic in nature, that is, a phenomenon of the figurational psyche, not of literal physicality, and to devise a method for accurately apprehending that representational nature entails an encompassing subjective effort of "recollecting" to the self-enlightening psyche more and more fully, in the words of esteemed lesbian Jungian Marie-Louise von Franz (1980), what has been "projected" as the symbolic dimensions of experiential life in the world, most so as the life of the mind itself. Persistent engagement in this subjective reclamation process creates something new in existential personal being of landmark qualitative status, a transformed and better-awakened self-consciousness increasingly able to take on moral authority and culpable responsibility for itself psychologically because it is thereby intensificationally rendered transcendentally to the conglomerating approximation of personally intimate terms with the universally divine, the key re-organizational step to a new power arrangement for all.

Such an internalizational political step historically emanates from, and empoweringly enacts, the new humanizational morality of the sacred that is pressing more critically on us now from an acceleratingly-agitated future, just as becoming homosexually identified does so, yet psychoanalysis cultivates focused applicational techniques that are unparalleled by any alternative approach, old or recent, in their locational capacity for particularizational self-engagement of that involving type most so aiming to better thoroughly expedite alchemical transformational becoming if pursued sincerely and persistently enough, that type of more-sophisticated technical approach which, not too many decades ago, was often being misused persecutorily against same-sex-loving peoples, but which now is seeing the start of more-liberated homosexual interest and activity, yet only today, with the efforts of the Institute for Contemporary Uranian Psychoanalysis, has progressive pursuit of gay-centered psychology and effectuational promotion of homosexual psychological awareness towards more-complete liberational fulfillment entered an ethically and ideologically coherent opportunity of systematically enhanced focus for cumulatively attaining a vivid degree of gay validation, exploration, and actualization entirely unheard of up 'til now. By comparison, it is not that, for example, Dr. Kilhefner's pronouncements calling for more same-sex-loving "adults" and "elders" are merely entirely unworthy, that so engaging the community in spite of the problems I mentioned before will not to some extent cultivate the way to better interior self-maturation. It is rather that such psychologically-ambivalent, homosexually-shallow ideological approaches to better-focused gay self-engagement, thereby render themselves inexpediently too self-compromising and thus deleteriously inefficient, increasingly so, it seems to me, as effective-enough change-agents in the stark face of today's burgeoning need for tremendous human and social modification overall, a Herculean reformational task vastly beyond that of, for example, merely stopping the worst sorts of sanctioned homophobic bigotry, or being able to use language that sounds gay-centered and psychological.

In other words, although both extravert and introvert modes of subjective functioning are equally important in human mental life, according to Jungian thought, it is the case that effecting better inward relational growth will conse-quently lead to better outwardly-oriented growth more than the other way around, and also that such improvemental inner advancement is best served by an authentic loyalty to full internal realization, most pointedly so at this fateful moral and political juncture for gay liberation activists and for the general human species as to where we can best invest for most-so maximizing our future survival and better success. Particularly as concerns the more-sufficient satisfaction of historical Gay Liberation as an indigenous Movement of inherent ethical and spiritual force ultimately sourced in and expressing a most-profound teleological intelligence of absolute individuational self-achievement homosexually and universally, the global moral call for a new human responsibility inevitably and com-plementarily requires an ethical gay psychology heroically aiming to wholesomely extend and sincerely complete the profound shamanic self-alchemy rightly unleashed qualita-tively by homosexual identity formation, a crucial internal extension of authoritative self-responsibility that progressively addresses the remaining blackened *prima materia* of retrospective traumatic effects still present needfully after a secure gay identity is salubriously well achieved, thuswise to transmutationally expedite more and more consequentially the finer chromatic truth of homosexual alchemical gold, a most precious jewel of the most exquisite sanctificational sort, a redolently scintillating boon eloquently sung of ecstatically and wondermentally by heartfully-transformed, same-sex-loving poets and sages of many famous and lesser-known cultures and eras, now to be made commonly available enhancementally to the good initiatory reach of all, the worthiest goal and cause that can currently be devotedly wholeheartedly served, in my humble personal estimation. Let us hope that boldly moving more purposefully into this brave new future of greater gay emancipation expeditionally through that resplendent subjective procreation which is today enabled best by cultivating a homosexually-centered psychoanalysis conscientiously, will rewardingly bear abundantly tangible access comprehensionally in an expanding qualitative manner summitorily to the estimationally rarest treasures and most-advanced constitutional marvels of possible human becoming, both for ourselves and for everyone. Thank you.

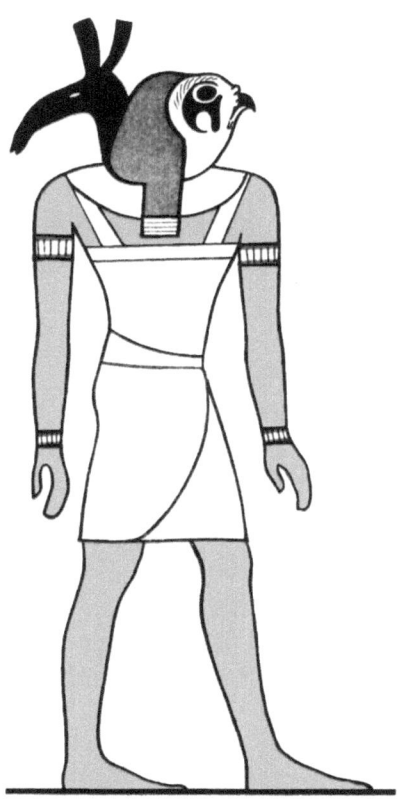

GAY LIBERATION AT A PSYCHOLOGICAL CROSSROADS: THE HISTORY AND DEVELOPMENT OF CONTEMPORARY URANIAN PSYCHOANALYSIS AS A PROGRESSIVE MARRIAGE OF GAY LIBERATION THOUGHT AND PSYCHODYNAMIC METHODOLOGY, ONE GAY MAN'S STORY

What is there after achieving a secure homosexual identity? After gaining the right to gay marriage? After all anti-gay laws have been adequately legally corrected? After homosexuals effectively heal the lingering psychological wounds of internalized homophobic trauma and successfully attain better loving relations with themselves and others? When every goal of the "gay rights movement" has been satisfied, and living as a valuable homosexual person has been rendered entirely, respectfully fulfillable, some say, there will no longer be a special need for gay liberation, community, or even identity, or that these factors will assume much less significance or distinctness, to be treated more like eye color or "ethnic background." We will all just be "people."

Such viewpoints could be described in terms of gay theory as strongly "assimilationist," because they ideologically presume no fundamental difference in being homosexual itself, only the unjustified stigma of social bigotry. Once that form of meanspirited scapegoating is removed, goes the reasoning, we same-sex-loving peoples will turn out to be pretty much like everybody else.

It seems to me that this type of vigorous assimilationist approach has come to dominate gay liberation ideology and politics in the homosexual community during the past generation, but there continues to be a vibrant alternative perspective about gay people arising from a contrary sensibility called "essentialism," which does not posit the end of gay liberation or personality with the fulfillment of the necessary war against social injustice, but rather the start of a new Homosexual Renaissance of maturational procreative excellence in being a valuable gay person with vital contributive import for the future of our very planet itself.

Indeed, in the mix of assimilationist and essentialist attitudes and feelings that I would suggest has always been present within homosexuals from the start of the modern Gay Liberation Movement of the past approximately one hundred and fifty years, it is the essentialist sensibility working in tandem with the desire to be treated equally that has most-so propelled the development of homosexual identity, ideology, community, and terminology, from our Movement's original founders such as the German Karl Ulrichs, the first individual to publically "come out" as same-sex loving and argue for a distinct "Uranian" person and justice-seeking minority, beginning in 1862, all the way to seminal American post-World War II activists like Harry Hay, principal co-founder of the first lasting gay organization in the U.S., the Mattachine Society in 1950, here in Los Angeles actually, who held that same-sex-loving folk constituted a discrete type of people with unique creative qualities and spiritual dimensions. Moreover, the contemporary gay rights movement itself is the direct historical outgrowth of a "post-Stonewall" liberational upsurgence which initially saw homosexual self-acceptance as progressing anywhere but to dissolutional integration into a social power system generally held to be of terminally corrupt and unjust constitution. Yet, not unlike what happened in the 1950s after the early achievements of the radical First Mattachine Society, that 1970s liberatory attitude's very conversional effectiveness unleashed a renewed urge to assimilate as well, leading to a reductionistic approach which has since come to ideological domination due to its increasing tactical success in a social world increasingly conservative yet not unreachable with acceptable appeals.

However, this growing integrative success, in concert with the diehard nature of persistent bigoted opposition, brings a tremendously pertinent focus to the key question of what does lie beyond self-acceptance and equality for today's Gay Liberation Movement. There is no disputing the need to humanize the perception and assessment of gay-identified people, and in that sense, gay liberation seeks assimilation into the "dignity of man" for homosexuals on a par with everyone else, and rightfully so. So there is a strong and valid side to the gay assimilationist impulse, that we are in many powerful ways, "just like everybody," yet if we follow a strictly, that is, one-sided, assimilationist perspective, what we will see is a relative "withering away" of gay distinctiveness, which prospect accordingly invokes a rather bleak and stultifying sterility as the likely procreative future of being specifically homosexual.

In the later part of his life, Harry Hay became quite concerned with this problem of the emancipatory homosexual future, and in fact, it was due to this interest that he, along with his partner, John Burnside, myself, and Don Kilhefner, co-founder of the L.A. Gay and Lesbian Center, began the Radical Faerie movement in 1979, in order to name, explore, promote, and moreso actualize both the humane dignity and the sacred potentiality in being abidingly gay.

Starting from even before the Radical Faeries but particularly since then, an entire so-called "Gay Spirituality" movement has emerged among gay men, featuring many prominent books such as Mark Thompson's *Gay Spirit: Myth and Meaning* (1987), Toby Johnson's *Gay Spirituality* (2000), my own early work, *Visionary Love* (1980), in addition to the magazines *RFD* and *White Crane*, and ongoing Faerie and related organizations and efforts by figures such as Christian de la Huerta (*Coming Out Spiritually:The Next Step* [1999]) in San Francisco, David Nimmons (*The Soul Beneath the Skin* [2002]) in New York, and Don Kilhefner as well as myself here in Los Angeles.

All these post-Stonewall essentialist efforts of a "spiritual" nature assess a prospective substantiality to being a homosexual person today of a portentous significance that must be better actualized both to gain a fully-humanizing gay liberation not sufficiently attainable realistically through a one-sided assimilationist route, and also to bring forth crucial creative and healing capacities desperately needed by the same-sex-loving community and the entire world.

This is the more-radical ideological direction, a gay-centered or homosexually-oriented direction, that would seek a renewal of our Gay Liberation Movement in the face of assimilationist successes and limitations by affirmatively deepening the appreciation of being distinctly homosexual beyond sexual behaviors, oppression, and words to abidingly essential qualities, characteristics, and possibilities of an authentic and distinguished sacred nature.

Of all these efforts to rebalance homosexual ideology by inclusively following out an essentialist perspective on our emancipatory future, however, only that of the Institute for Contemporary Uranian Psychoanalysis focuses on and makes paramount a careful psychological approach to homosexual essence, spirit, and personhood. The previous two talks in this series discussed why such a specialized method of introvert gay activism was being ideologically undertaken in historical, philosophical, and other terms, such as in terms of better addressing the still-festering consequences of internalized homophobia, in terms of the subjectively-stagnating limitations of a one-sided assimilationist stance, in terms of the pivotal evolutionary need of an emancipatory subjective morality to effectively take up personal psychological responsibility, in terms of a more active initiatory engagement with homosexual numinosity. All these interlocking explications were helpful ways to begin exploring how and why the gay community today is in a kind of internal dilemma over these necessitous themes, a psychological dilemma, and what then can be done to expeditiously address this difficult crisis, which is to deepen gay liberation theory and practice through enhanced psychological literacy, a project for which the Institute has been cultivating what it calls "contemporary Uranian psychoanalysis."

Now that this initial context has been set in terms of thematically introducing the larger topic of these talks, it would be useful to enter farther into what more particularly involves this newly-synthesizing enfranchisemental approach. Accordingly, tonight I would like to extend our explorations through looking at that specific historical development by which the method and formulation of a proper homosexual psychology has come, in its primary features, into present Institute comprehension, and in the following talk I would like to then detail a more-specific characterization of Uranian psychoanalysis today as "a homosexual realizational tool of bejeweling initiatory possibilities."

I would like to describe for you how an appreciation of Uranian psychoanalysis developed in me personally, a story which leads up to establishment of the Institute, as well as continues to this day.

As you can imagine, I was not at first inclined to be psychologically minded at all, of course, since I was a dutiful product of my out-of-it family, culture, and time as much as anybody else. Having been born in early 1951, nearby here down in Culver City, by the way, I was a true child of that famously conformist decade, and grew up in an oblivious world pretty much through successfully formatting a fairly oblivious attitude. Although I had always particularly loved experiences of the wonderful and magical—or "numinous," as Jung might say—which I encountered in the presence of animals and plants, dreams and fantasies, bright colors, movies, television, books, Disneyland, there is no telling if that might have been of sufficient interest in general to spark my later Jungian direction, because, starting when I was around eleven years old, I began to increasingly notice a particularly disquieting sort of marvelously intriguing reaction I was appetizingly feeling in the presence of certain male people, a peculiarly-warm upsurge that had actually been aromatically stirring for some years but which I had hitherto shied away from self-recognitionally specifying, an insurgent sensual upsweep that became growingly-so suffused with a lush intimational numinosity excitingly way beyond that of my love for animals or crystals, a most-savory kinetic feature provocatively highlighting a growing suspicion in myself which would fatefully come to dominate my inner ruminations and my actual future as a person, a professional, and an activist.

I did my best to keep warding off the doubts I felt looming darkly in my young self-consciousness, as I not-so-dissociatedly enjoyed the new genital sensations and imaginal beyond I was starting to pleasurably experience in spite of whatever shame, horror, or other malevolent reactions might have been lurking thereabouts. But by the time I turned thirteen, I had grudgingly come to vaguely sense that the accumulating evidence was unfortunately incontrovertible—I was experiencing a robust early homosexual adolescence in a repressive social world that despised and vilified such a focused amatory interest, violently and viciously. Finally, this bothersome self-suspicion then blossomed into clear recognition through an oddly singular and unanticipated incident of great force, as I continued clinging to what shreds of denial and dissociation I could in the face of my own intuition that a pivotal watershed was quickly approaching. One day, while I was walking to lunch in this foreboding mood with the rest of my seventh-grade class, across a street that divided our part of the school campus from the cafeteria, a vivid sensation of clouds parting came over me, and looking up, I heard from above a powerful, unfamiliar male voice boom out deeply in a measured cadence that emphatically and carefully spoke each word, "You are a homosexual!" It was not necessarily a judgmental or evaluative voice, but rather a factual one, yet with a personal sense of great profundity and implicative fate which, although quite immaterial and invisible in any literal sense, as I could see by looking around me at the unconcerned faces of my classmates, nonetheless had sharply jolted me like no single event I had ever encountered before, qualitatively more like something I could picture happening to characters in a fantasy novel or Cecil B. DeMille's 1956 religious movie, *The Ten Commandments*, not addressed specifically to me in a penetrating magical way such as I had never imagined could be individually actually available.

Needless to say, as they might have said back then, I felt "all shook up" pretty badly after that. I could hardly eat my lunch in the cafeteria that day for trying to better absorb what the voice had revealed and how I was then going to live a future life which was not to be privately only of hellish failure and pain, no matter its outward appearance. Naturally, I then blamed myself for this twisted condition, and I fell into a depressed state of deep mortification and toxic shame. What was I now to do? Undoubtedly this sticky quandary was not coincidentally unfolding during a period in my life when I was preparing for my Orthodox Jewish bar mitzvah, followed by its successful enactment inducting me into Hebraic male adulthood, and then my subsequent theological questions in *schul* being answered with repetitive suggestions to just keep engaging in the rituals and reading the texts.

Therefore, when the time inevitably arrived that I could no longer escape better accountability for the paramount driving question of what to do about my budding homosexual nature, I decided to turn, not to family or theology, but to therapeutic psychology, and seek better understanding there. At the time, I could not have said about this choice anything better than that it intuitively felt most accurate and hopeful to approach my problem from this more modern angle. So one night I asked my mother to arrange psychotherapy for me, as I had a big problem I didn't want to discuss with her but would with a psychologist. So she set up an appointment for me at the Child Guidance Clinic, and the older woman I met there several weeks later was the very first person I ever came out to as a "self-professed homosexual."

She was very kind and non-judgmental, and I was placed in a small therapy group with two other problematic boys and a nice male psychologist, but the other boys dropped out after a few sessions and the group was closed, so I just decided to keep winging it on my own after that, although I now felt more in touch with and understanding of myself following this first upfront encounter with a psychological approach.

For the next several years, I got along adequately enough as a deeply-closeted homosexual masturbator, while on the side I read as much as I could about gay love and personality, particularly where I could at my young age find psychological discussions, and I decided to myself become a psychologist in pursuit of greater comprehension in this amatory personality area that so intimately consumed me. Then when I was seventeen, the most confoundingly "catastrophic" of possible celebratory events heatedly overcame me, as I found myself, although I had had "crushes" before, unexpectedly falling in

love, romantically, sexually, and totally, for the very first time
with someone, somebody who just happened to be the handsome captain of our high school varsity football team, Herald
Rich. Just listen to that name poetically as it might be spun
out allegorically when so courageously venereally enflamed:
"The Herald of Rich Tidings," "The Richness Heralding True
Love," the thrilling homosexual metaphysical harbinger to
soaring qualitative wealth beyond all measure or compare,
the messenger of heaven on earth.

To say that in my inexperienced way I was utterly bowled
over by such vastly-intimating passion, would not have done
fair justice to the riveting adolescent revelations that freshly
kept marvelously rising up and up, scintillating in me. I was
transported, transfixed, and appalled. As this extraordinary
and consternating wonderment flowed on, I found that I
could not continue containing myself perfectly under the
consequent surging pressure of remaining otherwise so
expressively shut down and isolated in the protective fashion
which I had always been practicing since I first became
sexual, so I started an explicit journal of my flourishing secret
experiences, and when, after some months, that in turn grew
too much to keep similarly quietly contained, I determined
to give the journal to the object of my affections, who was
otherwise just a pleasant social friend, which I did out of the
blue after a shared social event one Saturday night, only to
be confronted by his appalled yet also caringly-concerned
reaction when I saw him next the following Monday at
school. He told me that he had burned my journal to ash in
the family barbecue grill.

This was the second time I came out to anybody. That
move subsequently led to a meeting with the school coun-
selor, who referred me to a prominent neo-Freudian, male
heterosexual doctor of psychology, with whom I thuswise
anxiously began therapy in the Fall of 1969, in a sincere

attempt to altogether "convert" my despised amorousness. Depressed, alarmed, and confused, I now self-loathingly hungered for a complete heterosexual "cure," and held only to the harshest judgment of my gay self, even though my first full experience of erotic-romantic love brought me so transfixedly into such an experientially riveting, ineffably inflaming *mysterium*, that I still feel thoroughly and thankfully gripped in its iridescent revelatory influence to this very day.

Finally, when I was 20 years old and still quite diligently working towards my seemingly endless cure, I found myself falling in love again, now with a friendly college buddy, and even though this passion too went unrequited, an unanticipated shift in basic attitude came over me that opened up a fathomfully new and revolutionary insight: Homosexual romantic love was actually a very good and special experience, not necessarily in any way morally wrong or spiritually bad. When my concerned therapist then only responded with indignant hostility and "caring" condemnation to my subsequent attempts at thoughtfully exploring what was for me a startlingly refreshing position, I soon decided to quit that therapy as now ethically bankrupt and instead start learning to authentically accept my actual eros and my resultant identity. I consequently step by step "came out" publically as a gay man, and in 1972 joined with some initial trepidation in the then-emerging, post-Stonewall Gay Liberation Movement, soon enough wholeheartedly embracing its to me now-wonderful emancipatory concepts and ideals. I there so became a proud and committed gay activist.

Still intellectually and existentially interested in better understanding my meaningful same-sex-loving origins and psychology, I would get into intense conversations with myself and others about the possible source and purpose of who we were as gay. Most of my new friends and associates, in understandably aversive reaction to homophobic oppression against gay people, were for the most part quite leery of even considering mental causes or subjective reasons. But having broken from the sickness model, I now hungered for more explicative illumination about my worthy homosexual self. As yet, though, I found little in the way of thoughtful literature or others' ideas that went very far past conceptual slogans like "gay is good," or being contributive gay versions of counterculture hippies or political radicals. I too had now become such a contemporary version, and this did indeed feel nurturantly inspiring and purposively fulfilling to an increasingly rewarding degree congruently light years past my prior self-denying existence, yet at the same time, my fundamental homosexuality itself in its deeper potential comprehension for me as a valuationally evolving person, still discordantly remained only a great big mystery, it did more integratively amount now to that central erotic and romantic fact which I eagerly stood fully behind, but for the most part all this was simply heterogeneously combined with the various other ideas, beliefs, and interests I along with my fellow activists experienced and followed.

It was in this fermenting context, during my 21st year, that I met Don Clark, the first openly-declared gay psychologist, whose sharply consolidated insights into a newly respectful apprehension of thematic homosexual personality I exhilaratingly found instantly galvanic, and from that initial encounter I avidly became his student. I appreciatively learned thereby to usefully apply gay liberation thinking to basic psychotherapeutic concerns, to gain a "gay-affirmative" or even "gay-centered" perspective about psychology, and in so doing I came to comprehend homosexual personality development in more respectfully mirroring terms of ably achieving a healthy gay identity and accordingly actualizing a qualitatively legitimate life of salubriously evolving selfhood integrally on that foundational incorporative basis, a modern humanistic view like that expressed by Carl Rogers' book, *On Becoming A Person* (1961), now appropriately concerned with and justifiably applied specifically to the essential moral dignity, valuational esteem, and creative fulfillment of the modern same-sex-loving individual as an authentically worthy, adult, sexual, and social being in freely-chosen affiliative association with like-minded others. Indeed, my own life exuberantly and delightedly now blossomed anew in the more sagaciously-incisive context of this novel comprehensional view, as I committedly worked under its facilitative guidance to more so claim and feel my body, sexuality, feelings, and sense of selfhood while I professionally trained to become a practicing psychologist and continued my rewarding gay activism. I wrote a master's thesis based on this regardful humanistic approach to homosexual people that eventually became *Men Loving Men: A Gay Sex Guide and Consciousness Book* (1977/1994). Now I was a progressively-emerging gay therapist and writer as well, and I even fell in love again for the third time, finally in a sincerely requited relationship of joyously-fulfilling mutual intimacy. It seemed to me satisfactionally that here I had at last really arrived at a truly better understanding of myself and the bigger meaning of my same-sex love, or at the very least an admirable start thereto, which promised a subsequent lifetime of amply fruitful progress in its more comprehensive unfolding.

Then, however, when I was 23 years old a surprise dual catastrophe fatally struck at this foretellingly happy picture. In the fall of 1974 my graduate school informed me that my almost-completed thesis would now be completely unacceptable due to an enhanced, detailed promotion of gay sexual fulfillment; I would have to write an entirely new thesis if I wanted to graduate. And then, seemingly coincidentally, my lover conflictedly abandoned our relationship to residentially return to his needy wife and two young children. I was plunged affectively into a deep cyanic sea of paralyzing confusion and bleak despair.

In this foully despondent mood, I became increasingly obsessed with what my lover meant to me, that I felt so amazingly hurt and yearning over his loss. Although I ruminated on a broad variety of interpretive psychological comprehensions as well as just plain stock notions, none of the many answers I came up with felt like it really explained things at all fully for me, or in any serious way satisfyingly calmed my stricken heart. Then one evening, I was aimlessly alone watching television in this grimly discontented mood, when I incidentally noticed they were showing a new version of the *Frankenstein* story. As I watched the tall, handsome young doctor electrifying his entirely bandage-clad creation, I noticeably started to get caught up in the old tale's basic magic and human drama. After he then turned off the juice, Frankenstein slowly stepped up to the now-breathing, mummy-like figure, and carefully started to unroll its long cloth wrapping.

I was imaginatively wondering what sort of variant makeup-engineered monstrosity would likely emerge from this supposedly tension-building little procedure, when, to my growing astonishment, the gradually unfolding bandage advancingly revealed, first, a very winning, boyishly handsome face, and then, as the wrapping kept going, a practically naked, lusciously hunky, reasonably muscular body. Finally, when the so-called "monster" hesitantly opened his beautiful brown eyes and sweetly smiled with such a touching look of innocent longing for simple love and compassionate acceptance, my own felt heart startlingly went into a bombshell meltdown at this confoundingly unexpected outcome, and I abruptly right then amazedly experienced an inexplicable apotheosis: The despisedly hideous creature I had completely expected instead dumbfoundingly stood winsomely revealed as himself a glow-ingly inviting angelman, a libidinal seraph of the heavenly Lord in gorgeous mortal form, a most powerful tantric instrument of effective embodying spiritual initiation. Later, I read that the teleplay for this version of *Frankenstein* had been written by Christopher Isherwood and his lover Don Bachardy (Smight, Isherwood & Bachardy, 1973).

Suddenly, in a sublime emotional uprush I felt all my own ugly pain and monstrous shame in the hurtful loss of my romantic relationship miraculously turn into their feeling opposites, and further with a ravishing scope of resplendent human meaning way beyond absolutely anything I could ever have possibly visualized before, and I now saw with an oddly piercing clarity that intrinsically within the encompassing erotic-romantic love I felt for my departed companion and all the others prior to him, whether gained or lost, there glo-riously inhabited accessibly a perpetually enthralling experi-ence of absolute awe and staggering wonder, of restorative magic, beatific spirit, sublime wholeness, and elevating tran-scendence only potentiatedly waiting just to be so feelingly discovered imaginatively and responsively explored passion-ately, a landmark revaluational experience about myself as personally homosexual of that distinctively-revealing type which, if even once tasted, will immediately be appreciably seen to be absolutely beyond all compare, and which could therefore in commendably estimable consequence be no less appraisingly affirming than if it overtly described intimate redemptive encounter with the ever-renewing presence of eternally illuminating God, or as I would soon discover in Jungian terms, the archetype of the Self in the evolutionary service of the maturational individuation process. In honest truth, the very soul of my own life has actually always been intently spent in rapt devotion to this radiant God of Beauti-fully Enlightening Love. Now I saw: Gayness itself was the sublime door to a still much better psychological understanding of my estimable homosexual personhood and its goodly qualitative possibilities vastly far past everything I had already rewardingly discovered and productively become up 'til then.

On that pivotal day of elevatory, earth-shaking revelation, I astonishingly met what seemed to be an inner autonomous intelligence perhaps configuratively akin to what ancient Egyptians called the Spiritual Witness of the Heart, and from then on he increasingly became a subjective guide and friend and teacher for me. He became the topic of a new master's thesis as one way I could then honor and more so understand him and this founding awakened connection to me within the felt beingness of my ongoing homosexual experience, whereby I interpretively explored the underlying symbolism of that epic motif I and all the other gay men I knew were so fascinated by and caught up with, the defining motivic theme of same-sex romantic love involvingly realized through mutual adult companionship with another caring man, in translational terms of the basic Jungian comprehension of genital love as being about the psychological "soul," meaning the interior source of felt aliveness and inspiration as specially erotically personified, in terms of which, if I considered the modern concept of reciprocal homosexuality at the most elemental level of sexual symbolism to refer to a genital pairing of like with like, suggested the apt metaphor of an erotic archetypal twin or double to one's own biological sex as the projectively sought-for wonderful companion, an alternative characterization of felt soul-relationship directionally operative in the subjective world of interior dynamic relations to that of a female-sexed figure in the amatorily patterning form of a primordially phallic "reflection soul," a resonantly-personal starting symbolism which I could then additionally amplify through various myths and tales of same-sex love both ancient and modern that analogously showed this reflective thematic pattern, such as found in Homer's *Iliad*, Plato's *Symposium*, the Old Testament, the epic *Gilgamesh*, *Franken-stein*, "The Secret Sharer," *The Lord of the Rings*, as well as many others. I then worked part of this exploratory analysis into a short paper, "The Double: An Archetypal Configuration," which was published in the journal *Spring 1976*. To my knowledge, this study was the first to ever appear in the Jungian literature by an out gay writer, and the first to openly espouse a homosexual archetypal point of view as psychodynamically providing a reasonable developmental basis for healthy gay love and salutary personality formation.

At the time of my overwhelming revelatory encounter, I instinctively sensed that to usefully understand it as a vividly-compelling *psychic* experience conceptually required a Jungian theoretical framework since, even though I knew of it only vaguely to that point, Jung's thought was the only sys-tematized approach to human psychology I was even remotely aware of which realistically offered to treat the fun-damentally numinous and stellar qualities of what I was sub-jectively going through ideologically in anything like a sufficiently respectful and sustained way rather than through reification, reduction, substitution, or other forms of what now seemed intellectually to me like hostile ideational manipulation or trivializing superficiality.

Therefore I eagerly turned to Jungian psychology and soon enough found that, while its hefty depth indeed mir-roringly satisfied what felt most important about the moral and spiritual gravity of my new personal revelations, its simultaneous homophobic devaluing of gays, and its exclu-sively heterosexual concept of a man's "soul-image," the alluring female anima, left me cold. But then it felt from my new gay-centered perspective, that by now positing a mas-culine complement in a man's psyche to the female anima in order to account for the marvelousness of my exaltational experience as constituently involving something necessarily on a qualitative human par with heterosexual romantic love as traditionally analyzed, yet not at all adequately enough described morally by any standard Jungian concepts of gendered archetypes and relations, I could then easily enough picture the practical development of a compelling homosexual soul-figure complex on such a phallicly personifying basis as being symbolically behind the waxing value I and other gay men intoxicationally felt about same-sex romance, as being of a reciprocally-interested nature distinctively different in various featured dimensions from analogous love for a woman, yet similarly personably gender-oriented and suchwise just as ethically profound and spiritually full of treasurable valuational portent in its own relational way for our benevolent substantiating progress toward satisfactionally reaching a healthy psychological maturity, as a determinative erotic love self-referentially for the same sexual gender interactively on the most richly human and ethically humanizing scale of sincere mutual intimacy and commendable subjective growth, as an ultimately-mystical and initiatory "object love" of and by the masculine sex that also includes its own symbolic form of adequately experiencing and wholesomely incorporating the psychic feminine as well, and thus so, as comprehensively involving in its own justifiable right that key actualizational process of integrational psychological advancement Jung calls subjective individuation. On this equitable syncretistic basis, I could then understand the simple mental image of one's own biological sex, generically-considered, as now itself constituting an inner representational personification which could then be metaphorically said to be the personal twin or archetypal double of one's physically-embodied sexual gender, accordingly in men an inner penile "brother" to the contrasexual anima as vaginal "sister," and with whom through heartfelt homosexual romance, wholesome personal relations with the archetypal psyche could go generously verdantly forward via salutarily operative soul-figure dynamics. I called my resulting master's thesis *Gay Depth Psychology*.

In discovering this novel symbolic understanding homosexually, I felt sweepingly transported into a newly encompassing dimensionalization of expansive universal value and motoric substantifying purpose—both psychological and political—regarding estimable gay love, identity, and liberation. Jungian analysis, in addition to generally appreciating the modern humanistic idea of subjective self or what I might here call *personhood* that I had already incorporated from my earlier studies, goes daringly further within that respectful intellectual tradition to take completely seriously the phenomenological experience of still-deeper symbolic meanings, of the strange and amazing mythic and mystical dimensions, of that veritable magic and transcendental spirit which most emphatically reside energically within the livingness of human subjectivity itself, those specially glowing features of life's meaningful experience which preciously hold our deepest values and highest ideals, where the sincerest fundamental truths and august wonders are finely well forged for the salubrious actualization of necessary human possibilities through the hallowed constitutive process of inestimable self-realization, ultimately the worthiest fulfillment or completest fruition knowingly of that core human "soul" referentially understood to be the archetypal source of all life and vital inspiration in felt subjective experience as the truly finest flower of richest awakening personhood, a marvelous, uplifting sensibility I had always intuitively been quite sweetly drawn to, even after disgustedly ceasing to be any kind of religious believer at the volatile age of 13, but that now stood freshly revealed in thoughtful erotic horizons of fantastic mythical grandeur and unfathomable human potentiality.

What well psychologically amounted to an enlightening union of my homosexual identity and the initiatory archetypal psyche, fruitfully mediated interiorly by my conceptual discovery of a gay-centered Jungian synthesis, honestly-speaking felt simply ecstatically miraculous, an epochally satisfying alternative to both traditional spirituality and modern secularism in becoming and being a fully-meaningful human person who was sincerely liberatedly same-sex-loving.

As Jung might say, I suchwise came entrancedly under that marvelous influence of the awesome *numenosum*, the towering transcendental power of the psychic archetypes, by phasic developmental degrees relationally to a fuller scope of purposeful meaning and irresistible feeling entirely unanticipated, which then drew me to investigate through apposite analogy to parallel figures from the historically-recorded past how it seemed amplificationally that the homosexual spirit-power had actually been previously widely recognized as a great magician and mystical guide, a powerful shaman, a masterful alchemist and expert transformer of the elemental stuff of psychic being, the inner world, the dreamtime, the spirit land. Plato and the Orphics called him Eros, Egyptians named him Tajuti, Sumerians, Enki, European alchemists, Mercurius. I accordingly discovered him to be not only a beautifully sexy man, but also a universal wheel of mystic fire, as well as the realizationally completed Sacred Androgyne who there so incarnatedly holds the pivotal mystery of the cosmic opposites, the "secrets of life and death." This great originative enigma was what driven Dr. Frankenstein zealously sought to solutionally answer in the bold experiment to make his autogenetic creature, this indeed was the noble mystical goal of King Gilgamesh's heroic journey across the poisonous waters of death after his loving partner had miserably died. And this is likewise what I also most arousingly felt I was really revelatorily pursuing in my gay Jungian explorations, the very-most secret of essential homosexual life.

I became quite richly inflated unconsciously with these meaningfully grand notions of a mythic "origin story," accordingly revelling in soaring rhapsodic union with the concordantly-aroused transpersonal almost as if I was myself a god-like being, and so naturally enough such a lofty personal identification before too long not-unexpectedly (except for me at the time) then consequently resulted in just as substantially big of a valuational fall. I excitedly rushed to complete my new thesis even as fresh words kept tumbling out in a giddy surge, so going on further to now finish a larger manuscript still more ambitiously called *Notes toward a Gay Psychology*, of which "Gay Depth Psychology" was just the penultimate chapter. After this big opus was soon enough finally completed, however, a peculiar and unexpected change affectively set in. Seemingly for no reason and with increasingly alarming frequency, I started experiencing surprisingly-difficult panic attacks while in regular social situations, and presently a quite dreadful feeling spread through me that these puzzlingly-commanding subjective assaults emanated from a mortal enemy of immaterial constitution who was thus so now actually implacably hunting me down personally, an unyielding demonic being or force who demanded no less than my very death. I intellectually knew that these growingly tangible fantasies were not of course otherwise "real," yet, as they autonomously assumed increasingly heated form, I inexorably grew to ominously conclude that, by my having so involvingly "played around" investigatively with what I had inductionally discovered to indeed be the very real powers of the independentally living psyche as so sweetly seduced by homosexual romantic love richly valuatively amplified through respectfully contextualizing Jungian thought, a much greater awesomeness had truly been therein activationally very materially individually summoned which was in stark existential fact no longer in any moving way ecstatic, but instead quite horribly queasily baleful. Now I felt it ruthlessly closing in on me more and more tightly, and absolutely nothing I tried doing to ward off this otherwise-fantastical, squeezing doom made any practical difference. I only grew increasingly preoccupationally terrified.

Fortunately, at a certain straitened point I then, in another intuitive burst, desperately turned to a man who would become, along with his longtime companion, one of the first out gay persons to be certified as a Jungian analyst, David Stockford, and entered systematic analysis with him. There I gradually learned to protectively manage and engagingly partner the fiercely threatening experiences hotly irrupting from my agitated psyche, which as I did this now unanticipatedly proceeded to alchemically transform me from the inside out. Through such an authentically pursued *inner work*, I compositionally underwent that profound self-initiation of the substantive re-constitutional sort which ancient Egyptians analogically likened to the sun's transfiguring passage generatively through the twelve gates of the baneful underworld at night. I thereby learned full well that my first approach to Jungian psychology and its idea of ensoulment had been mainly just apt words and progressive concepts, indeed that my entire engagement with psychology and even myself until then had been but only a suitable-enough preparation, and now I was unmitigatedly shown the far-more-tangible reality of what Jung called the "objective psyche" in no uncertain revelatory terms, through what onerously amounted impactfully to an earth-shattering confrontation with the still-unresolved unconscious conflicts, steep moral inferiority, horribly incapacitated feeling, and their tremendous transpersonal implications which Jung characterized metaphorically as the dim "shadow" of one's conscious ego personality. My resulting initiatory education was most thoroughly rectificationally convincing.

As I devotedly worked through and so progressively deepened my inner process of this transmutational self-engagement during the next several years, I saw myself gradually move away from my earlier professional associations and also from foregrounding formal theory, to instead more directly explore the improved psychological embodiment of gay archetypal actualities as I wholeheartedly took up a whole new direction in my everyday pragmatic life. I became a sort of novice shaman and acolyte alchemist to what I now idealistically considered realistically to be an archetypally-sourced Gay Spirit and its beneficent evolutionary unfolding in myself and communally. Eventually this fresh comprehensional approach led me to produce a new series of formulational essays published in 1980 as *Visionary Love: A Spirit Book of Gay Mythology and Transmutational Faerie*, and to my friendship with Harry Hay, which began in 1976.

Harry, a seminal figure in the early American Gay Liberation Movement, was the first man I ever met who seemed to appreciatively see into those wonderfully depthful reaches of vibrant Gay Spirit and consequent gay-centered understanding which I had also discovered psychologically so feelingly through my cumulative alchemical initiations in becoming a better-realized homosexual person, and on that deeply warm basis, which Harry fully reciprocated, I immediately felt intimately bonded with him fraternally to more so explore gay male self-realization as an archetypal and political truth in the better actualizational service of our greater human liberation and finer enriching fulfillment as upright gay individuals and a distinctive gay people in caring contributive relation with the worthy whole of humankind. In this germinative context of growing affectionate fellowship on such a regardfully extended scale of caring mutuality, I discovered the rich inscribed history of that gay-centered thought first introduced to me by my earlier political activism and beneficial association with Don Clark, that is, homosexual writers overtly exploring the basic nature and possible meaning of gay identity and a homosexual perspective as the source of existential being and epistemological knowing, in modern times most notably from Walt Whitman and Karl Ulrichs (and their precursors) through Edward Carpenter and Gerald Heard to Harry himself, and now to my own budding gay experience and intellectual practice. This great cultural tradition is the main historic source of today's "gay identity politics" and its "ethnic" homosexual consciousness (see Roscoe, 1996), it provides the intellectual spine for the modern Gay Liberation Movement and all we have justly achieved as gay people. Now proudly intending to help carry this noble cultural tradition farther into the new emancipatory terrain of a gay-centered myth of initiatory subjective meaning, Harry and I along with John Burnside and Don Kilhefner publicly called together the first Spiritual Conference of Radical Fairies in 1979, which has since spontaneously given birth to a grassroots type of ongoing world-wide religious movement.

In eagerly working with Harry and the other Faerie activists to actualize Gay Spirit more extensively, however, I unfortunately soon enough discovered disconcertingly that there was very little practical appreciation for the psychologically-unconscious shadow side of human subjectivity which I had come to realize was really quite omnipresent intransigently, such that, as would always be the case, everybody unreflectively tended to simply act out psychologically from their unprocessed inner defenses and complexes in extraverted group situations with deleterious results and no attempted self-awareness, in spite of a generally-proclaimed allegiance to gay archetypes and gay mind. It turned out that I was the only one of the organizers present who had attained any serious psychological understanding of such distaff moral matters as defensive re-enactments present ubiquitously in the operative subjective moment. When I would then try to conscientiously raise such crucial concerns with my fellow organizers, no matter how carefully and self-revealingly, I was regularly met by dissociated obliviousness, defensive attack, hostile projection, and shameless denial. Yet I consequently found that I could now ethically no longer, as I more or less had self-justifyingly done before, simply continue to go along with the anti-conscious collusion persistently being implicitly demanded of me (as of everyone in such manipulative group contexts), so eventually I really got to encounter the collectively-manifesting gay shadow as well as how that impressive interpersonal difficulty in turn experientially moreso provoked my own strong feelings and psychological issues, as unconscious group dynamics coalesced to oppose my subsequent concerned expressions of increasing apprehension and then rising anger. Harry, in particular, not only absolutely refused to even consider any psychological understanding of who we were and what we experienced and did, but now even loudly proclaimed that any such understanding would be murderously anti-gay and thus morally anathema! This was after several years of my activist organizing with Harry during which I and others observed him persistently to act out dehumanizing themes of bullying, castrating, and controlling other gay men with a competitive domineering enthusiasm, while being very "fae" about it, that perpetually refused to acknowledge any responsibility if anyone protested.

This ugly organizational quandary within the Radical Faeries schismatically arose because, conscientiously through my ongoing initiation into serious psychological inner work consistently pursued since the age of 18, I had more and more cognizantly come to honestly discover the true unresolved scope and terrible thwarted depths of toxic shame, crushing pain, infuriated hurt-rage, and other related noxious feelings lastingly injuriously engendered traumatically from my own formative past that were developmentally still needing to be fully faced, ably processed, and engagingly integrated psychologically so as to successfully fuel my own fuller healing from bitter homophobia and other poisonous influences that had without my sensible awareness stunted more fathomful actualization of my estimable gay personhood and better valued potentials, and in then dutifully responding to that core diagnostic discovery, I richly well experienced the materializing birth of a redemptively greater relationship with the homosexual transpersonal within me as I also perceived with much enhanced clarity the entirely-pursued extent to which I and all others quite actively colluded in covertly or unwittingly dysfunctionally re-enacting traumatic psychological business while secretively maintaining thorough conscious avoidance of the darkly-injurious actuality of inflammatory unconscious conflicts through all our otherwise-sincere mutual efforts unless insidious personality defenses were rigorously systematically challenged. It was in responsibly attempting to effectively bring my deepening awareness of these vital psychodynamic and relational issues apparently so influentially bearing on more-successful subjective liberation to my principled activist work and participating personhood in the homosexual Faerie movement, that I educationally saw the truly pervasive power of iniquitous psychological defenses so strongly fanatically provoked in otherwise decent people as supposedly aware individuals and in purposeful constructive groups, and through which I very helpfully and somewhat painfully gained, in the light of such reactionary controversy, not only a respectfully enhanced appreciation for the pivotal need, amazing potential, and epic challenge of usefully integrating an honest psychological attitude with gay liberation theory and practice, but also of how very much called for just such a synthesizing activist step was politically in important moral contribution accountably toward better realistically solving the seemingly intractable problems of terrible violence and rapacious injustice that are today woefully still so rampantly unrestrained powermentally in the human world at large.

As I persisted with these gravely consequent concerns interactionally among my fellow Faerie activists in the difficult organizational context of a deepening conceptual and personal schism, I was finally able to get through communicatively to another Faerie cofounder, Don Kilhefner, who also then more seriously began to thoughtfully recognize the historic usefulness and major importance of liberatorily learning to better actively appreciate the elsewise hidden psyche, and together when we saw that Harry and others would now do all in their aroused power to oppositionally block any more-direct exploration of gay psychological understanding, we frustratedly resigned from the original group and in 1982 founded an alternative educational institution still operating today called Treeroots, to focus specifically on estimable gay psyche and its more growthfully-unfolding psychological self-encounter through workshops, talks, and publications.

Don Kilhefner was an original member of the Los Angeles Gay Liberation Front in 1970, and worked with Morris Kight to create the L.A. Gay and Lesbian Center, the first of its kind, in 1971. He was brought into the initial Radical Faerie circle by Harry, just as I had somewhat later recruited Mark Thompson, another important early activist, yet Don became deeply disillusioned with Harry's unconscious acting out. After he then joined with me to focus on the work of gay psyche, he went back to school along with me (at his suggestion to strengthen our work) and has since become, like myself, a licensed psychologist. But I found over time that, in our collaboration together, he would not endeavor to become more emotionally honest and authentic in relating to me regarding his psychological defenses and issues as key actualities needing real and specific engagement in the spontaneous moment between us, instead staying coldly closed off, keeping such matters tightly "private." Since I now increasingly held that working for deeper psychological authenticity in intrapersonal and interpersonal relations, particularly regarding shadow dynamics, needed to be purposefully foregrounded by all subjective parties present methodologically to make better substantive progress along the valuational lines of further potential gay liberation, our relations thereby grew increasingly strained until one day in 1984, when Don and I were alone in his apartment for a meeting and he suddenly and unexpectedly hotly and viciously accused me of having stolen important ideas of his, such as that of studying a series of gay men's dreams for a doctoral dissertation (we were both in graduate school together at this time). When I protested that I thought he was misinterpreting my interest in entering a more substantial intellectual dialogue between the two of us, he grew yet more hostile and suspicious, finally denouncing me bitterly as a user and exploiter of others. From that time on he was condemnatorily distant but polite to me, and we only spoke together formally regarding Treeroots business, if at all, until Don eventually resigned from the corporation in 1995 and founded a new organization that was first called Tumescence and now the Gay Men's Medicine Circle.

This split with Don, as I considered it, appeared to echo that with Harry earlier, in that Don seemed to be responding to a similar challenge to the usual rulership of psychological defenses as if he had something deeply complicit to protectively hide, by lashing out accusatorily and then righteously disowning our association (when I had first directly raised this issue with Harry several years earlier, he in turn had instantly walked away vociferously accusing me of wanting to supplant him). Don has since gone on, as some of you may have noticed, to a public career as a spiritual leader in the Los Angeles homosexual community that includes the ongoing demonization and trivialization of myself and anything to do with me historically and presently through shameless lies and distortions, while prominently claiming himself to be shamanic, psychological, psychotherapeutic, and Jungian, all four features of which career he initially learned about in any important way from his association with me, as I had been and was, from the time we first met, practicing these particular comprehensions as such when he wasn't even very familiar with, much less doing, any of them, nor was anyone else in our associative activist grouping. Such exploitational and dehumanizing measures suggest to me unself-examinedly being in the unconscious grip of overweening feelings of envy and rage followed by guilt and fear or even terror of getting caught if the perceived threat of culpable exposure for ruthlessly acting out such nefarious motives is not fiercely obliterated, a terribly infantile, anti-psychological stance also suggestively echoed in more recent years by Don's extraverting articles in *White Crane*, *Frontiers* and elsewhere, as I have more extensively discussed in my last talk, articles by him which camouflagingly mimic the inclusion of a psychological attitude by occasionally referencing apt terms like "archetype," "dream," "ego," and "soul" so as to appear up-to-date in regard to what really counts most these days, while in more immediate actuality something else entirely unprogressive is covertly working its violent, exploitative will.

Such schismatic developments with Don, although challenging, underlined for me again just how powerful and radical an authentic psychological direction was for future gay activism, and I consequently felt additionally-confirmed appreciation for the helpfully guiding utility of a deeper exploration theoretically into homosexual thematic dynamics and distinctive personality growth as categorically amorously gay.

After first developing the basic idea of a subjective gay soul-figure as representatively amplified by an archetypally-based double image, I then spent the next few years exploratorily practicing "in the field," so to speak, experientially delving shamanically into enhancingly-vibrant metaphors of numinous gay-centered archetypes, culminating in the Radical Faerie movement and the book *Visionary Love*, before finally returning intellectually to again formally reconsidering Jungian theory as the best methodological way to usefully approach a more realistic homosexual subjective comprehension and consequent better political emancipation, now with a much deepened appreciation of myself, gay-centeredness, and the amazing and often confounding workings of the dynamic unconscious mind. The written result was my doctoral dissertation in 1987, *A Uranian Coniunctio: The Individuation Model of C. G. Jung as Applied to Gay Men*.

In that study, my theme was to further articulate the masculine double as commanding soul-figure, how it could specifically work functionally as the archetypal love object in meaningful gay romance actively pursued toward gaining something crucially worthy, how this homosexual soul-complex in an interactive dance of mystical erotic twinship with the amorously cooperative ego could better than adequately operate a gay man's valuable subjective individuation generatively to and beyond the defining hallmark achievement of a stable gay identity and the verdurous adult capacity therewith for mutually gratifying love. While in my initial study of the phallic double as motivational soul I had been theoretically concerned primarily with archetype as thematic content, here I became more-so interested in archetype as a kinetic process of unfolding intrasubjective relationship, and in particular, with uncovering the possible sentient nature of a homosexual-centric libido in the Jungian sense of the autonomously intelligent dynamism inherently present within the fundamental "substance" and diverse activities of manifestational psyche. In proposing a sapient homosexual form of psychic libido's basic organizing intent, its purposively guiding Eros, I thus discovered I could conceptually reach a much more basal level in appreciatively understanding gay psychosexual dynamics, the reasonable figurative comprehension of a gay-oriented "informing intelligence" at determinative compositional work in all the active libido's doings, its formative constellation of the personal complexes, its motivating experience of the originative parents, its propulsive shaping of the ego identity, its elementary transformation symbolism, its miraculous transcendent function, an ideational revolution of perspective in considering basic Jungian notions about human psychological growth. Thus, for example, an expressively emergent Homosexual Eros in a man would functionally constellate the masculine double as determining soul-figure and the feminine anima as romantically congruent ally, while a comparably forming Heterosexual Eros would likewise unfold the thematic object-relational reverse.

Earlier Jungian views had merely "naturally" assumed a heterosexual perspective on the part of organizing Eros, the inherent intelligence of genitally-directed love. Now with such novel, respectfully transgressive notions as I have just mentioned, gay liberation thinking accordingly arrived at the inner sanctum of rigorous analytic thought: the theory of the libido and its constructive transformations. I called this imagined figure of the homosexual libido's originative developmental intent *Uranian Eros*, after Plato and Ulrichs, and then systematically followed out from there various apposite metaphorical associations to suggestively show his improvemental alchemical operations in the ongoing incorporative enactment of a Uranian "sacred marriage" or *coniunctio* with the responsive ego personality elevatingly up a transmuting Divine Ladder of the elemental Sacred Heart in refining qualitive development of valued gay personhood through a cyclic propulsive Haunting by a homosexually entrancing Wraith-Buddy Soul, consequently leading constructively through both improved differentiation and enhanced integration of conscious and unconscious psychological being from the original auspicious birth of rousing homosexual romance to an indescribably transcendent goal, the ultimate ethical purpose of maturational human existence.

In my dissertation research, I had compared the contemporary experience of successfully reaching a secure gay identity with Jung's expository treatment of a series of arcane pictures from an ancient European alchemical treatise called "Rose Garden of the Philosophers," which show the passionate union and subsequent transformation of the alchemical King and Queen, to Jung the growthful encounter between ego and unconscious. I, in turn, then investigatively interpreted these allegorical figures as analogously showing a receptive proto-ego fatefully encountering its authentic homosexual unconscious, yet the resulting analysis did not leave me feeling entirely satisfied. I wondered why I had told a story of homosexual development through a patently heterosexual imagery. Also, that story had thematically focused on protean libido's advancing vicissitudes from puberty on, without addressing the formative kind of childhood dynamic which would account for the later configurative rise of gay adolescent sexuality and romance.

The more I pondered this puzzle, the further I found that a thickly obscuring fogginess would come over me, such that I was forced to patiently engage in sensitively relating actively to this thickly stubborn resistance for quite some time. But after many months of such actively-efforted inner "cooking," a crucially-loaded association finally popped up: I suddenly saw an image in my mind that glowed intensely with an intangible light of all colors, an oddly florescent picture of my father as a young married man standing in front of my first home looking at the camera that had somehow been recalled from an old black and white snapshot I had once seen long ago. Then it dawned on me just how out of it I had been about this problem, that actually here I was thematically confronting a homosexual sort of "filthy mystery" of the especially discrete sort which Jung was always associating with heterosexual erotic love and the soul complex—genital incest and the "family romance." Now things quickly fell into more understandable place: A basic wish for father-son incest swept up gay boys phallicly in a shaping equivalent to that illicit desire conformingly moulding the heterosexual Oedipal complex, compelled thuswise oriently by Uranian Eros as the "ruling divinity" from the very beginning, thereby inevitably leading to an ambivalent identification with mother and the entire unfolding of a defining personal configuration necessarily metaphorically involving both originative parents of one's existently-incarnated being, a homosexual familial romance, by which a responsive proto-ego in effective working tandem with a likewise-emergent homosexual soul and his lusty amorous pursuit into serious adult love could be well organizationally constellated to therewith formatively actualize an androgenously-integrative personhood. With this bright idea of a homosexual "filthy mystery," something not at all ideationally heard before, radical gay liberation had coherently reached even that arcane secret *mysterium* theoretically resident within the Jungian sanctum.

I came to formulationally call this gay domestic motoric configuration the *Uranian complex*, just as I had similarly characterized the subsequent adult unfolding of worthy romantic interest as based on and occurring through the symbolic patterning dynamic of an alchemical Uranian conjunction. Now I could return to the already-worked analysis in my doctoral dissertation and expansively "fold in" this underlying formative theme of homosexual libido's emblematic incorporative childhood to portray a more-complete mythical story of humanely personalizing Uranian Eros successfully operational in constructive gay individuation, thereby uncovering the wily incestuous secret of those transubstantiating efforts by which he cleverly achieves a full gay selfhood, and likewise by which he can be fully homosexually well known psychically. With this advanced ideational clarification of a divinely royal *mysterium* constituently present alchemically in the constitutionally formative encounter with commanding gay romance, I felt I had truly and honorably redeemed the shameful "filthy secret" of my own pubescent sexual awakening, I had indeed comprehensionally discovered a starting metaphorical lead that resultantly became preciously meaningful gold.

This revised investigative study was then assembled with several of my Jungian papers and a newly written Introduction into a book manuscript in 1996 called *The Uranian Soul*.

Meanwhile, Treeroots activism had been continuing into the 1990s on the part of various engaged participants in addition to myself, people such as Chris Kilbourne, who had become my partner in working towards better homosexual self-awareness starting in 1979, Mark Thompson, who was an editor at *The Advocate* when I recruited him into the original Radical Faerie organizing circle, probably around 1980, and who later became himself an important leader in the community, as well as Doug Sadownick, currently director of the LGBT specialization in clinical psychology at Antioch University Los Angeles, and Roger Kaufman, author, therapist, and educator, who both joined in the early 1990s. Then, starting in 1996, in a developing situation that eventually mushroomed into a firestorm of reaction, an associate of various Treeroots activities began openly accusing Mark of likely infecting him with HIV at irresponsibly-operated educational gatherings, a charge that Mark vigorously objected to.

At first, I gave little credence to the possible accuracy of such accusations. Then, the more I considered the situation, the more other people began approaching me, spontaneously and unbidden, to mention other events and also the ones under dispute which they had witnessed or reliably had heard about where Mark had indeed appeared to behave in unsavory and distracted ways, with the result that what had at first seemed more clear now became much less so. When I then attempted to address this problem in a final face-to-face meeting with Mark, he vociferously again completely denied the validity of any negative comments about his behavior with an aroused tone which seemed to me noticeably quite defensive and even frightened. After I pointed out that he appeared to be reacting psychologically in a very big way and then inquiring into what was going on for him, our subsequent exchange quickly devolved into Mark basically dissociatedly fleeing the room mentally in the forceful confrontational face of my insistent focus on thoroughly addressing the matter, and we finally parted with no resolution other than Mark conciliatingly agreeing with me in a seemingly half-dazed manner that he needed to face something in himself better. Since then, Mark has completely separated himself from anything related to myself or Treeroots, even going so far as to recently say, according to someone who was present, that when we had known each other, I had been a mere "acquaintance"!

In fact, it is interesting to further note that after each important organizing figure, Harry, Don, and then Mark, reactively dissociated from developing an authentic psychological attitude, each later reached a rapprochement with the others, as shown, for example, in Mark leading workshops offered by Don's group, the Gay Men's Medicine Circle, awhile back, and also in Don frequently reminding people, as in his more-recent *Frontiers* article on "The Radical Faeries at 30" (Jan. 27, 2009, p. 51), that it was principally he and Harry who founded the Radical Faerie movement.

The confrontational situation with Mark Thompson wound up outlining for me all over again the steep challenge and remarkable power of seriously taking up a homosexual psychological attitude in how Mark, as had Don and Harry before him, in the end appeared to defend his defenses "to the death," as they say, rather than fairly accept accurate responsibility for them. While I was willing in each case both to acknowledge my own feelings and actions in light of my private psychology and to broadly recognize everyone's individual "right to privacy," I was not willing with any of these persons—or with anyone if I can help it—to just, as Mark put it in his final note to me, "agree to disagree" about giving carte blanche to violently act out on other people one's private psychodynamic issues, including the collusional forcing of others to submissively agree with such defensive forms of malicious acting out, instead of vigorously exposing and openly dealing with those predatory dynamics all the way to their causal roots.

The fierce hypocritical behavior of these three leaders is reactionarily typical of the psychologically uninitiated when faced with gravely-embarrassing exposure, and I see similarly juvenile sorts of petulant ultimatums and other dramatic maneuvers commonly in my psychotherapeutic practice. At the same time, these activists' dour regressive consistency suggests the specific psychic ravages of profound homophobic bigotry as well as the onerous task of functionally breaking from the one-sided extravert bias of socially trained externalizing, a protectionist locational prejudice seemingly more doggedly stifling in society today than ever. I myself originally likewise existed arrestedly in the terrible psychic grip of such suffocatingly traumatic and regressive forces, and similarly I have many times seen in my almost-40 years of doing counseling and therapy how it is quite possible for somebody to victoriously break that multi-faceted defensive grip homosexually through the most challenging and profound of measured self-initiations systematically wrought by sincere and persistent inner psychological work.

Therefore, in regard to a minimal level of sound capacity for psychological self-awareness and ethical responsibility absolutely necessary historically at this more-advanced level of emancipatory subjective challenge, adequately functional leadership for the next stage of gay liberation theory and practice obviously requires a much more serious training in homosexual psychological authenticity and the contextual literacy required for this new capacity, such that it would inevitably be the case that an appropriate institution accordingly should be set up responsibly for this pioneering invocational purpose, conceptually underpinned functionally by an appropriate ideological formulation.

This latter step began to more particularly concretize for me first with an initial circumferential statement in 1999 called *The Revolutionary Psychology of Gay-Centeredness in Men, Three Short Essays*, and then more comprehensively starting in late 2002 with the death that October of Harry Hay. I noticeably felt in my imagination that an ethereal call had been sent out by his passing to augmentationally imbue my 1996 book manuscript with a deeper stylistic voice of newly synthesizing scope evocationally very far beyond that normally to be otherwise literarily expected, such that by the time I was well underway in this stylistic memorial endeavor of eventually four years, I could see that its growing cohesive thrust, formulative detail, and fae sensibility nicely set the descriptive stage comprehensionally not only for my own current efforts as a gay activist, practitioner, and person but that of an increasing number of well-committed and -tested fellow participants, such that the arrangemental basis seemed adequately set ideologically to now propose, on a coherent formulational basis, the definitional establishing of an operating scholarly and professional facility with a succinct descriptive name to referentially encapsulate this novel homosexual liberational effort, the "Institute for Contemporary Uranian Psychoanalysis."

As I point out in the Introduction to the renewed version of *The Uranian Soul*, subtitled "A Gay-Centered Jungian Psychology of Male Homosexual Personhood for a New Era of Gay Liberation Politics with Universal Implicational Import," in activist moral terms of the necessary human liberation of gay-identified men from hateful homophobia to be and fulfill themselves to the finest substantiating extent they can reach toward, the particular facilitative power of considering important issues from first a psychological, and then specifically a Jungian, view lies in a more effective retrieval of the gay-identified individual to the raw immediacy of his own gay psyche and to its infinite qualitative riches, the sheer goodness of more authentic being, and through that fundamentally enhancing estimation, to the immeasurable wealth of the prospectively living archetypes, the inner primordial forms of universal evolutionary truth. Systematic humanistic approaches which can broadly be called "psychodynamic" and "psychoanalytic" aim to facilitate realistic agential access to encountering the existent private reality of living human subjectivity in its better-maturing actualizational possibilities to the most profoundly-specific extent attainably available today, it seems to me, and by usefully thereso formulationally situating ultimate spiritual, erotic, and political truth within valid gay identity itself through such carefully-differentiated, psychoanalytically-informed self-access, the homosexual individual is in this singularly-empowering way thuswise ethically promotionally authorized and qualitatively estimationally ennobled, at the most fundamentally-imminent grassroots level, constitutively through self-reflectively so knowing his own intimate psychology redemptionally to thereby best realize enfranchisementally his worthiest valuational potentials. In the elemental improvemental encounter between, and evolving capacious integration of, desirously seeking ego and evolutionarily personalizing psyche that is expansively engaged relationally within the developmental subjective domain, bounteously lie the fulfillingest human depths of all immortal import, as I have amply discovered experientially and as classical Jungian psychology clarifyingly articulates, the root archetypes of pure absolute Meaning and vital cosmogonic Essence, thus easily capable resourcefully of ably well actualizing a magnificently virtuous profundity of most estimable Gay Spirit in seriously useful doing and delightfully existent being which is not only well estimationally beyond all oppositional doubt and questioning debate, but even more so importfully, which is actually capable enzymatically of advancingly changing whole worlds. To intentionally better aid such a majestic transformative process more effectively through this maturative sort of expansive homosexual self-understanding, amounts to a basic ideological theory and systematic engaging practice designed for pointedly focusing and helpfully nurturing meaningful gay liberation of and in the vitally-experienced psyche with a vastly enhanced immediacy accordingly opening politically onto an entirely-new scale of resultant impactful effect, a cultivatedly purposeful politics and applicationally practical technology focusedly facilitational of improved homosexual

existential self-becoming and worthwhile personal empowerment that could consequently be described as an activist
or contemporary "Uranian psychoanalysis" that catalytically
enables consciously more-liberatorily "coming out inside" so
as to properly enact fulfillmentally a transmutational "gay
soul-making" of the richest revaluative possibilities, and such
a Uranian psychoanalytic approach thuswise harbingers a
fundamental contextual advance in homosexual "identity
politics" that I regardfully believe can momentously lead to
a further political stage in modern gay history and even
world history.

This new comprehensional advance carries the enlight-
ened tradition of emancipatory gay-centered thought into
more expediently engaging and productively navigating the
sourceful inner sanctum of its own self-awakening subjectivity through importantly-resonant psychodynamic terms, into
insightfully regarding contemporary homosexual personhood
in consonant accessing terms of its inner configuring Origins
and prospective Final Outcome—not only a tremendous
ethical improvement over the hatefully homophobic use of
psychology and psychoanalysis just a few years ago, but even
more crucially, a signal humanizing step that seminally opens
gay-centered entree to those momentous methodological
tools by which the inwardly-relational objective psyche can
be most fruitfully encountered existentially in an increasingly
unrestrained and finer facilitated process of archetypal Self-
realization as a commendable gay person.

Such a progressive, aimful approach to the causal nature,
mythical composition, and transvaluative possibilities of subjective human being as homosexually salubriously informed,
in complement to other dimensions of both psychological
understanding and gay-centered thought, experimentally
enacts a novel formulative combination practically concerned
with more so helpfully understanding and harnessing, in the

context of a general "affirmative" psychoanalytic regard, what can through Jungian psychology be secularly appreciated to be valuationally eternal and qualitatively transcendent specifically about gay-identified psyche when supportively channeled better effectively towards the laudable goal of amply reaching meritorious personhood's full-fledged humanization and best auspicious possibilities, with thus so relationally engaging those deeper subjective resources nurturantly associated to powerful symbolic aspects of homosexual psychological life most so allegorically involving fertile encounter with the archetypal Self, the "greater personality" within— because in the end it is actually numinosity itself that really moves humanity, and it is the fundamentally felt *spirit* and *soul* of subjective existence that makes anything at all worthwhile—, what amounts to a momentous new type of liberatory political analysis of richer subjective self-realization which then brightly casts in an expansively-revealing light not only modern gay personality development but also the historical Gay Liberation Movement as well, its causal origins and profounder purposes, and from that watershed insight to the additional suggestion of a greater untapped but increasingly-needed homosexual ethical potentiality widely present actualizably among humanity overall, the possibly-crucial political relevance of which may only be additionally magnified governmentally as the current social era of epochal corruptive transition and consequent persistent crisis inevitably discordantly continues to haltingly ambivalently unfold.

Therefore, in terms of the fundamental historical question of what lies ahead for being coherently same-sex-loving in the light of those assimilationist and essentialist themes I laid out at the beginning of this talk, the personal and ideological story I have now told you will hopefully give you some idea of one way that this challenging but outstandingly opportune predicament can be seriously tackled today, the way that has led to contemporary Uranian psychoanalysis and the three-year-old Institute founded in its name. This is how some of us are attempting to conscientiously address in a productively timely fashion the pressing political crisis of viable homosexual futurity which is stalking our community and movement today, and we wholeheartedly invite you to join with us in this bold new leap to more-direct gay liberational psychological honesty, awareness, responsibility, exploration, empowerment, initiation, metamorphosis, maturation and beyond, toward a revolutionarily-refoundational renewal transfigurationally for homosexually-identified personhood, and community, and indeed the wide world altogether. Thank you.

GAY LIBERATION AT A PSYCHOLOGICAL CROSSROADS: THE COMPOSITION AND SCOPE OF CONTEMPORARY URANIAN PSYCHOANALYSIS AS A HOMOSEXUAL REALIZATIONAL TOOL OF BEJEWELING INITIATORY POSSIBILITIES

As I previously explained in the first talk of this series, I believe that the Gay Liberation Movement today faces a signature theoretical and practical challenge due to accruing assimilationist success combined with the persistent momentum of internalized homophobic bigotry, what momentously amounts to a fateful choice for current homosexual ideology, to either continue as is and increasingly creatively stagnate, or instead take up a serious psychological attitude toward fuller liberational completion of valuable gay personhood.

In the second talk, I described how it was that anybody taking up a non-superficial psychological direction will soon enough be inwardly assaulted by fierce defensive resistance, and without a concerted commitment sincerely dedicated to complete psychological honesty and responsibility within a supportive ideological context, no great progress could be made in this formidably novel task of deepening homosexual authenticity. Therefore, a corresponding comprehensional and functional approach to effectively addressing that virginal emancipatory requirement needed to be systematically cultivated, articulated, and institutionally supported by good gay effort, thus leading to the formulation of contemporary Uranian psychoanalysis and the organization of an appropriate facility dedicated to this model political endeavor.

In the third talk, I then entered moreso into the particular nature of a Uranian psychoanalytic approach to Gay

Liberation's present generational quandary by relating my own personal story and struggle to apprehend same-sex desire, love, orientation, identity, and liberation psychologically, which efforts have in concert with those of other committed activists led to establishment and current operation of the Institute.

We saw how I was taken on an imaginal and intellectual journey of a lifetime into better grasping what I came to think of as "gay-centered psychology," that is, the substance and perspective of same-sex-loving psyche, how I first discovered a humanistic understanding of wholesome homosexual personhood from my apprenticeship with Don Clark, the first declared gay psychologist, which then led to a self-confrontational "dark night of the soul," culminating in my more direct encounter with homosexual archetypal numinosity and subsequent attempt at an explanatory comprehension theoretically focused on the innovative Jungian notion of a phallic companion soul or transpersonal double.

These fresh revelations brought on a hefty inflation and its subsequent loss that sent me into Jungian analytic therapy, from which I gained a whole new degree of valuable alchemical initiation through revelatorily thoroughly facing the terrible trauma in my own shameful shadow-side within a transpersonally appreciative context.

Such a worthy personal reformation allowed my gay thinking to subsequently go through further formulational developments in Jungian synthesis to produce the notions, which I outlined moreso in my first talk, of an archetypally-causal intelligence within homosexual desire, Uranian Eros, an early developmental stage of homosexual family romance in incestuous parental triangulation, a Uranian complex, and an understanding of gay identity formation in terms of homosexual romantic love as an alchemical engine of self-becoming personhood, as enacting an operational Uranian *coniunctio* or transforming sacred union which has progressed through one-third of its full growthful arc with successful confirmation of a secure gay identity, the personal realizational arc altogether of a radiantly transcendent Uranian soul.

As well as leading to a more-advanced line of homocentric analytic reasoning, my alchemical self-confrontation in Jungian therapy brought about the maturational context in which I first met Harry Hay, the chief instigator of the original Mattachine Society in 1950, and therewith I discovered the intellectual tradition of gay-centered thinking that Harry was very appreciative of, which was also a crucial factor in my subsequent Jungian reformulations.

However, in then working closely with Harry and other gay activists to start and continue the Radical Faerie movement, which aimed for a populist summoning of homosexually-centered consciousness, valuation, and spiritual exploration, I came up against the egoic psychological defenses covertly ruling people and their interpersonal relations when psychological awareness is absent and uncultivated, and when I rather naively attempted to question this all-too-typical stranglehold arrangement among the Faerie organizers, defensive resistances were impressively marshaled against my attempted efforts.

It became necessary for me to learn to struggle effortfully over a long time with what turned out to be a persistent interpersonal problem, most importantly first with Harry, the principal authority within the original Radical Faerie organizing circle, then later with Don Kilhefner, co-founder of the L.A. Gay and Lesbian Center, with whom I had eventually broken away from Harry in the face of Harry's persistent anti-psychological hatred, and still later with Mark Thompson, the author and editor, who had stayed loyal to me when Don had viciously attacked me as a vampiristic user when I kept pressing the issue of being psychologically authentic. In Mark's case, as I related in the last talk, an eventual parallel failure, as earlier with Harry and Don, to accept the interior source of strongly felt provocations when repeated charges of unsafe-sex practices were levelled against him by various sources, in my estimation led to wholehearted merger with primitive psychological defenses of splitting and dissociation, followed by vigorous, self-justifying accusations and complete ostracization unless I "agreed to disagree" with him on the acceptability of violently acting out unconscious defenses irresponsibly.

And, by the way, in relating to you these gay organizational stories of others' personal relations to me and what I did about it, I do not wish to imply in any way that I myself was simply some sort of innocent, sweet, Buddha-like figure participatorily in all this, that I was not having my own shadow issues, defenses, projections, and actings-out going on that could well have been contributing to the overall problematic situation, for example. Indeed, I certainly could become defensive, attacked by inner shaming voices; I could intimidatingly approach someone in terrible fierce ways that could only gain their angry forcefulness from channeling strong early traumatic complaints, and so on. But I do feel I was also sincerely attempting, as I still do to this day, to consciously be aware of my living shadow reality, to take moral responsibility for it, to not obliviously exploit others as an easy method to scapegoat my own infantile pain and need for revenge, to always try seeing the other point of view, and to learn by my own self-scrutiny and shameful mistakes, and accordingly such a faithfully-attempted psychological attitude is what, I would maintain, makes my instigation of and participation in the interpersonal leadership developments I relate of a unique functional order to that important historical organizational progression in an instructive fashion which I have attempted to equitably and accurately document by way of these talks.

Indeed, it was my repeated confrontational encounters with fellow gay organizers that brought home to me so impactfully just how crucial the moral issue of personal psychological responsibility is, practically speaking, particularly for those who have been the unjust objects of brutally-traumatic social bigotry, and generally for a collective human world resistantly one-sidedly much too extraverted, the subject of the second talk in this series. Unless all of us can learn to accurately perceive and account for our private psychodynamic processes sufficiently as a pivotal authorial act of directional energic rebalancing, we cannot relate to others as actually separate beings nor to ourselves as anything other than a self-justifying chimera. This is the stark subjective consequence of that historical group-vs.-individual politics emancipationally unleashed by the unstoppable rise of radical Enlightenment humanism which has been shown to me so thoroughly, first and foremost by my own self-encounter in ongoing inner work, and secondly by my interpersonal relationships with other gay activist organizers in addition to those with other participants, clients, and so on over the past 40 years.

Therefore, the gay introversional comprehension aimed for by the theory and practice of contemporary Uranian psychoanalysis, as it pertains to any truly subjective topic, would have to start with an overarching contextual appreciation for the actual reality of the experiential psyche and with its sincere self-relational engagement. Learning to be authentically "real" and more fully present in one's psychological moment is in my overall experience a lifelong developmental challenge and internalizing journey which most so amounts significationally to that crucial moral task set us seasonably by the epochal march of personal subjective liberation, a pressing reconstructive task powermentally that, in my opinion, in situational terms of our present day and age, cannot be duteously escaped except at terrible cost, indeed, that very cost which is cumulatively bringing our fair planet to the brink of ecological catastrophe and a most massive species extinction.

As such, I feel it is every human being's ethical duty to learn to take better responsibility for her or his personal psychology, and it is this accountably conscientious perspective which most clearly morally separates a truly new age of human being, doing, and becoming from that of the old, an aeonic transvaluative shift towards legitimizing subjectivity as paramount politically amounting to a signature reformational imperative which, in my estimation, a defensively-externalizing humanity cannot ultimately keep avoiding, as it shamefully has in the past and presently on the whole continues to do.

Thus, the historic liberational way of reconfiguratively developing personal authenticity properly becomes evolutionarily an ethically requisite path of honest confrontational self-realization psychologically, through which valuable and necessary subjective transformations are to be maturationally attained authorizationally, no matter who you are, but especially in impactful regard to having been painfully oppressed homosexually, and we will keep this orienting valuative appreciation well in mind as we now consider the more-complete developmental fulfillment of gay psychological personhood.

In order for same-sex-loving folk to cultivate and employ subjective authenticity effectively, requires a suitable methodology and attendant ideology within a gay-affirmative framework, and this is, then, the functional context for syncretistically marrying psychoanalytic methodology to gay liberation thinking and homosexually centered appreciation in a manner that broadmindedly incorporates a range of general therapeutic understandings such as the recovery and embodiment of feelings in the moment, integrative processing of infantile trauma including on affective, somatic, and ideational levels, reprogramming dysfunctional mental habits by applying cognitive-behavioral techniques, and verbally engaging with others about subjective dynamic issues to learn better about interpersonal and internal openness, honesty, and trust in psychological matters.

So we might call contemporary Uranian psychoanalysis a gay-centered, coherently-organized process tool or set of tools borrowing from various useful psychodynamic conceptions for the sake of accurately learning to be moreso embodied and present in the psychological moment as a proudly self-identified homosexual, not just in terms of the reparatory psychotherapy situation but as a progressive way of living life as an authentically self-respecting, growth-oriented homosexual human being. In taking up a gay liberation attitude, Uranian psychoanalysis posits the rightful achievement of good gay identity as the first decent step in a life-long reclamation sequence of valuable self-recovery as a regardful same-sex-loving person, a necessary appreciation of full gay liberation subjectively that aims for the greater beauty and empowerment of deeper homosexual self-realization.

This attitude towards complete gay humanization means taking advantage of the entire panoply of apt psychoanalytic formulations for addressing dysfunctional personality dynamics related to issues of trauma, intimacy, trust, and so on which injuriously appear in one's life generally and in the spontaneous moment, in order to operationally pursue subjective homosexual recovery and better estimable development ongoingly with oneself and with likeminded others more effectively. Most notably, I have found it means responsibly taking up a sincerely and persistently cultivated relationship with one's own living psyche, and I mean this in the classical Jungian sense of cognizant intimacy in its particulars with what exists in the experience of being. "As above, so below," said the First Alchemist, Hermes Trismegistus. That is, just as we perceive a vast universe outside subjectivity, so too can we discover its full equivalent, if you will, a "little universe," inside self-perception. This was the approach taken by Jung: to observe and seek informed connection to the "objective reality" of one's own subjective psyche as autonomous, motivational, and of the most-profound possible richness, as with the external world.

So, when a securely gay-identified person sincerely works to seriously address the ethical challenge of the psychological moment, there is the necessary building of more involved and cognizant relations to the homosexual psyche, which better-forged connectedness can then be strengthened and advanced moreso by applying an appropriate Jungian frame of reference and tools of engagement such as active imagination, dreamwork, and symbolic amplification.

Thus we come to the overall significance and usefulness of a Jungian comprehension to the better facilitation of gay psychological actualization, which, as I have described in each of my prior talks in this series, concerns Jung's appreciation for the transcendent and teleological in the human psyche, a catholic regard that, in spite of his own homophobic limitations, can be empoweringly extended to overt homosexual self-realization. Indeed, due to this particular aptness of Jung's thought for a better grasp of valuable gay becoming, moreso even than that parallel insightfulness to be gained by applying, for example, psychoanalytic self psychology to issues of homosexual trauma and healing, is it the case that a contemporary Uranian psychology would recognize the overarching relevance of taking up a disciplined analytic approach which is both theoretically rigorous and gay-centered, while also reparationally allowing for the eclectic practical and theoretical features I described before as a liberatory "set of tools."

Today, let us explore further how such a systemic Uranian extension of psychoanalytic activism can be applicationally undertaken in terms of specific Jungian techniques. Although in my previous talks, examples and illustrations of a gay-centered Jungian synthesis were being variously provided, now I would like to delve into this syncretizing process a little more specifically. First, I would like to focus on that method and attitude Jung called "active imagination." As Barbara Hannah, the lifelong lover of fellow analyst Marie-Louise von Franz and a devoted friend of Jung's, said of this approach, "if we honestly want to find our own wholeness, to live our individual fate as fully as possible; if we truly want to abolish illusion on principle and find the truth of our own being, however little we like to be the way we are, then there is nothing that can help us so much in our endeavor as active imagination" (*Encounters with the Soul*, 1981, p. 12).

This method consists of learning to be sensitive and receptive toward, and better relationally engaged mutually with, the spontaneous fantasy expressions in images and feelings of the dynamic psyche within, exploring by contemplative and active means how to tune them in, partner them seriously, discern their concerns clearly, follow them out dialogically, be taken interactionally more and more thereby into differentiated encounter between the conscious and unconscious sides of the vital, procreative mind, meaning the ego works to stay separate and a partner to the fantasy life being feelingly so experienced and conversationally so engaged. Particularly for gay people, important healing issues of the wounded self will need to thus so be reparatively located and interactively worked out through effortfully directed relatedness with one's inner infantile themes as if they were childhood metaphorical voices, one's "kids," for example, as aspects of one's "gut feelings" for oneself, or patterns thereof, arising from early traumatic wounding, developmental thwarting, and so on.

However, real engagement with the objectivity of one's own psyche must become a two-way street, in that the better-awakening gay ego in turn learns from and is transformed by this growing mutual intimacy with the unconscious reality. A greater sense of autonomous clarity and personal wholeness begins to emerge, along with the eventual discovery through that budding interior completeness of personal gay relations to a qualitatively-greater meaning, the meaningfulness of the transcendent. Thus is tangibly born a new, individually sourced and transpersonally felt "myth of meaning" to follow as homosexual rather than other symbolic stories of one's gay origin, purpose, and ultimate result which are believed in because of outside training or other external determining influences.

From this analytic point of view on personal growth, all humans exist subjectively through and in the medium of myth, that is, symbolic meaningfulness, and everything that is or can be subjective is symbolic or mythical in this sense, that is, as representing something qualitatively greater which cannot be conveyed in any literal way, and that in terms of this essential symbolic meaningfulness of subjective existence, everyone is socialized in a manner that vampiristically steals from individual psychic empowerment through enforcing the inevitable internalization of collectively-governed group identities such as "the family," "the religion," "the nation," and so on that limit and defuse who and what a person can personally be, what is their ruling myth of meaning, not just for those singled out by a particular social bias, but for all, with deleterious effects on the inevitable need for more completely singular individuation as life fulfills itself.

From this perspective, one can also see being homosexual and gay-identified as myths of meaning in terms of social categories, and then these myths too will need to be better individualized. But unlike the collective identities I alluded to above, existing as gay starts from the inside out, and is based on a sincerely felt passion of commanding endogenous definition. This, as I have indicated in previous talks, makes gay people an unusual sociocultural group in terms of that identity and affiliation, such that a gay identity is not merely social or collectivist in origin, but possesses an indigenous ensourcement allowing for the completest possible individuation of personal homosexual identification, in a manner analogous to how Jung has described further subjective evolution as heterosexually identified. In that regard, we should not allow contemporary postmodern, queer-studies, and other supposedly-progressive critics, on top of traditional homophobes, to again deny us same-sex-loving peoples the potential value and grandeur of deeper psychological becoming as homosexual along the amorous transformational lines Jung has boldly alchemically charted for straight psychology. Therefore, to the extent we homosexual folk can grasp hold of the analytic tool of active imagination to work at taking up a more-liberating gay story or humanizational myth of meaning as same-sex loving, the more we can help bring that better-satisfying realizational fate about for ourselves internally and externally.

Because in this series of talks I have been careful to summon the dark and difficult aspects of progressively seeking more-consciously-enhanced homosexual individuation, today I would like to summarize this necessary appreciation for the distaff side of salutary gay psychic growth in proportion with visionarily imagining what a better-developed future might advantageously hold in store for valuable homosexual personality. Indeed, to summon the auspiciously more-mature possibilities of humanistic gay becoming against the deleterious assaults of homophobic depersonalization not only enacts a righteous rebalancing but an encouraging promotion of gay appreciation to that august level of qualitative assessment traditionally delivered by Jungian thought to prospective heterosexual functioning.

Such a fair elevation in the dignity and signification of same-sex love and personhood is long overdue, and I see it as one of the main duties invested in contemporary Uranian psychoanalysis and its supporting Institute to bring forward such a freshly-enriched appreciation for more-advanced gay valuation, for a more-serious inner alchemy of that symbolic "little universe" where exists the self-respecting yet shadow-ridden gay ego and its homosexually-marvelous transformational potentialities.

It is from having achieved the inner personal strength of a secure gay identity which is preliminarily aware of and productively engaged with its autonomous psychic unconscious through vigorous same-sex love, that the functional basis now practically exists for the realistically-useful apprehension of the transpersonal Homosexual Beyond that fatefully awaits in the fecund depths of the gay-identified psyche.

With this subjective relational context now empoweringly well-established, such a conscientiously-growing, same-sex-loving person has already successfully begun an ongoing developmental practice of active imagination in the Jungian sense with his living gay psyche, just not in a more self-reflectively aware and purposeful manner, yet a viable preparatory connection thereby well readied for better introversionally undertaking a more-involved transcendental journey of good homosexual becoming.

Let us now enter on that further enhancemental path ourselves a little today by invoking some apt symbolic imagery using relevant Jungian methodologies.

I invite you to envision having a personal inner relationship with gay fantasy and feelings of sexuality, love, identity, and truth that magically becomes a profound transmuting expedition into most-treasurable qualitative becoming.

Holding on to this vision through the remainder of the exposition, let us now employ an additional Jungian tool, amplification or informative comparison to analogous motifs from other times and places, to stimulatively suggest what such a valuable journey could lead to, for the sake of imaginatively having a more progressive relationship to that psychic possibility at this moment and into the unfolding future. For example, in my book, *The Uranian Soul*, I relate how the rich fantasy life of a gay man dying from AIDS, Alfredo, came to strongly resemble or suggest to me an ancient Gnostic story of enlightenment called the *Hymn of the Pearl*, in which a man with a lost soul is redeemed to his heavenly brother in an act of being bedecked in a beautiful, wondrous robe. The scholar Hans Jonas explains this redemptive metaphor as concerning

> the "figure of light that comes to meet the dying," also called "the angel with the garment of light." In our narrative [of the *Hymn of the Pearl*] the garment has become this figure itself and acts like a person. It symbolizes the heavenly or eternal self of the person, his original idea, a kind of double or *alter ego* preserved in the upper world while he labors down below: as a Mandaean text puts it, "his image is kept safe in its place." It grows with his deeds and its form is perfected by his toils. Its fullness marks the fulfillment of his task and therefore his release from exile in the world. Thus the encounter with this divided-off aspect of himself, the recognition of it as his own image, and the reunion with it signify the real moment of his salvation. (Jonas, 1963, p. 122)

Here is that story in the *Hymn of the Pearl* as translated by Dr. Jonas:

They created the messenger and sent him to the head of the generations. He called with heavenly voice into the turmoil of the worlds. At the messenger's call Adam, who lay there, awoke...and went to meet the messenger: "Come in peace, thou messenger, envoy of the Life, who hast come from the house of the Father. How firmly planted in its place is the dear fair Life! And how sits here my dark form in lamentation!"Then replied the messenger: "...All remembered thee with love and...sent me to thee. I have come and will instruct thee, Adam, and release thee out of this world. Hearken and hear and be instructed, and rise up victorious to the place of light." (p. 84)

...

My letter [i.e., the messenger] which had awakened me I found before me on my way; and as it had awakened me with its voice, so it guided me with its light that shone before me, and with its voice it encouraged my fear, and with its love it drew me on. I went forth... [and m]y robe of glory which I had put off and my mantle which went over it, my parents...sent to meet me by their treasurers who were entrusted therewith. Its splendor I had forgotten, having left it as a child in my father's house. As I now beheld the robe, it seemed to me suddenly to become a mirror-image of myself: myself entire I saw in it, and it entire I saw in myself, that we were two in separation, and yet again one in the sameness of our forms.... And the image of the King of Kings was depicted all over it.... I saw also quiver all over it the movements of the gnosis. I saw that it was about to speak, and perceived the sound of its songs which it murmured on its way down: "I am that acted in the acts of him for whom I was brought up in my Father's house, and I perceived in myself how my stature grew in accordance with his labors." And with its regal movements it pours itself out wholly to me, and from the hands of its bringers hastens that I may take it; and me too my love urged on to run towards it and to receive it. And I stretched toward it and took it and decked myself with the beauty of its colors. And I cast the royal mantle about my entire self. Clothed therein, I ascended to the gate of salutation and adoration. I bowed my head and adored the splendor of my Father who had sent it to me, whose commands I had fulfilled as he too had done what he promised. (p. 115)

Here is a different translation of a section of the story describing the Robe of Glory:

My bright embroidered robe,
With gold and with beryls [emeralds],
And rubies and agates
And sardonyxes varied in colour,
It also was made ready in its home on high
And with stones of adamant
All its seams were fastened;
And the image of the King of Kings was
    depicted in full all over it,
And like the sapphire stone also were its
    manifold hues.
And again I saw that all over it
The motions of knowledge were stirring
And as if to speak
I saw it also making itself ready.
(Mead, 1960, pp. 412-413)

Here is some marvelous and powerful imagery for homosexual metaphorical stimulation, especially when we consider
that such ancient myths themselves can be appreciated, as
Barbara Hannah and Marie-Louise von Franz point out, to be
"prototype[s] at the root of the later individual technique of
active imagination" (*Encounters with the Soul*, 1981, p. 22).
What then do you suppose it imaginarily could mean to
"ascend to the gate of salutation and adoration" in today's
context of valued maturation of good gay personhood?

Such a mythic enlightenmental rise to heavenly divine
relationship also occurs as a central metaphorical motif in an
even earlier and more famous story, that of Socrates' climac-
tic revelation in Plato's *Symposium* of his spiritual teacher
Diotima's cardinal philosophy of amorous love, which is the
passionate experience of wonderful beauty, and

> he who from these ["ever-growing and perishing
> beauties" of the mortal world] ascending under the
> influence of true love, begins to perceive that
> [divine] beauty, is not far from the end [of his journey
> into the "mysteries of love"]. And the true order of
> going, or being led by another, to the things of love,
> is to begin from the beauties of earth and mount
> upwards for the sake of that other beauty, using these
> as steps only, and from one going on to two, and
> from two to all fair forms, and from fair forms to
> fair practices, and from fair practices to fair notions,
> until from fair notions he arrives at the notion of
> absolute beauty. This…is that life above all others
> which man should live, in the contemplation of
> absolute beauty, a beauty which if you once beheld,
> you would see not to be after the measure of gold
> and garments, and fair boys and youths. …[but after]
> the divine beauty…thither looking, and holding con-

verse with.... Remember how in that communion
only, beholding beauty with the eye of the mind, he
will be enabled to bring forth, not images of beauty,
but realities (for he has hold not of an image but of
a reality), and bringing forth and nourishing true
virtue to become the friend of God and be immortal, if mortal man may. Would that be an ignoble life?
(Plato, trans. 1956, pp. 378-79)

Here again we have the metaphor of ascending to heaven
and becoming the friend of God. In addition, the more-
detailed idea of "step by step" is introduced, thus suggesting
stairs and a "ladder to heaven."

The analogy of a spiritual developmental ladder is actually
very widespread, and we can see this transformative pattern
in such mythic motifs as the Hindu kundalini chakras, Jewish
Kabbalistic sephiroth, and European alchemical operations.

Let us follow out an example of working with this ver-
tical staging pattern in gay-centered Jungian synthesis, taking
a specific metaphor of sequential alchemical operations as
imaginally amplifying on the journey of valuable gay becoming in symbolic terms of a "union in heaven."

Already in the previous amplifications that I just cited,
much richly-stimulative figuration was summoned for the
path of homosexual ego-psyche developmental relations, in
that, for example, simply relating to the idea of one's feelings
of romantic same-sex love as a bejeweled living robe can
become a daily meditation of superb active-imagination possibilities towards better homosexual individuation. Since we
gay people have been so badly condemned and denied, our
need for the homosexually auspicious and treasurable has
been terribly starved, such that supportive and encouraging
fantasization in this wondermental internal direction is
appropriately to be warmly caringly welcomed.

So, if we would like to go farther in stimulating good gay possibilities subjectively, we might consider imaginative amplification of appropriately more-detailed parallel metaphors, as I do in *The Uranian Soul* by comparing Vivienne Cass's six-stage model of homosexual identity formation (Cass, 1979) to the twenty operational stages of a medieval alchemical pictorial sequence found in a book called the *Rosarium Philosophorum*, or, "Rose Garden of the Philosophers," the first ten pictures of which show a royal King and Queen meeting, having intercourse, dying, and fusing into one mystic corpse called the *Rebis* or Hermaphrodite, followed by its triumphant resurrection in the tenth image, a thematic sequence strongly resembling that of a growing gay child approached by upwelling homosexual interest, subsequently affectively inundated thereby such that the old way of being, identity, and belonging dies away in the struggle to successfully then internally accept one's same-sex-loving feelings and resultant identification against oppositional homophobic condemnation, such that a greatly renewed valuation and wholesome integration of estimable self as appropriately homosexual is nurturantly satisfactionally achieved. Thus, I likened accomplishment of a proud gay identity to the resurrected *Rebis* of the tenth *Rosarium* picture as Jung had traditionally treated it, as showing a fundamental advance in personally incorporating previously split-off shadow material enabling a wealthful enhancement in self-presence, -clarity, and -validity holistically likened to a silvery lunar Empress of All Honor, that is, the sound achievement of a good gay identity as manifesting a better refined connection to the Original Intent within subjective existence, which Jung called the archetypal Self. This notable accomplishment occurred through the establishment and growth of a homosexual soul-figure or phallic double imagined to consist, like its ancient Egyptian parallel, the *Ka*, of seven pairs of constituent qualities or aspects from the most basic to the furthest advanced, whose constitutional maturation amounted to a substantiating developmental ascent up a seven-rung ladder from the ground of mere gay potential to the "perfection in Heaven" of effectively uniting with centralizing same-sex love at the core of a secure gay identity, a kind of bejeweled enrobement.

Here is some of how, in my book *The Uranian Soul*, I describe the first ten *Rosarium* images as a mythologizing amplification of successful gay identity formation:

"By a magnificent revaluational Perfection of the greening dioscourian Romance is it viably so particularizationally that a divinely alive Rebis of treasurable Uranian identity authentically manifest delimitationally in groundedly-good feeling and locationally-framed thought assuredly is wholesomely gestated compositionally and well birthed substantializationally in a contemporary gay man's healthfully evolving psyche as symbolically comprehended methodologically by our respectfully-depthful exploration, it meaningfully amounts thereso to an androgynously integrative union between himself and his vital soul partner which then triumphantly constitutes self-empowermentally an initial necessary step compositionally toward that inestimable redemptive resolution completorily of those prominently-influential parental complexes and inferior Shadow self that we reasonably pictured to have been configured endogenously by distilling constellation of a lineamental Uranian complex in the foundational beginnings of coherent subjective being. That is, a young gay boy spontaneously falls into genitally-organizing love passionately with his hotly phallic father at the appropriate developmental point, and he thereby facilitatively sets in delineating motion through this numinous entanglement a fatefully confirming crystallization of inner emblematic imagoes of himself and his parents as the chief symbolic actors

in a secretive private narrative of most-important metaphysical meaning, his aboriginal Family Romance, the complica-
tional terms of which then develop those lodestone personal
complexes of the amorously arousing double soul, with its
yearned-for heavenly promise and transgressionally castrating
reversal, beneficently exhilarated Aphrodite Urania, with her
strong protective wisdom and vigorous controlling domination, and the nubile child self of best heartful hopes and most-
sweetly-valued dreams, who receptively experiences while
growing up all his primarily-unfulfilled homosexual needs
and contradictory feelings vis-à-vis these valent symbolic
parents, the painful inferior emotionality of his own darkly
Shadow self. The symbolic transformative Perfection of
homosexual archetypal romance, therefore, psychologically
entails the full working out resolutionarily of these Uranian
object-relational tensions emancipatorily in the usefully-
evolving subjective domain, and with estimable establishment
authorizingly of valued gay identity in the illustrious White
Rebis of the benevolent lunar Empress of all worthily known
Honor, metaphorically-speaking the thwartedly wounded son
is thus so nurturantly redeemed to the good blessing mother
and in consequence so leading pleasingly to a beneficent synthesizing integration rectifiedly of the basic gendered opposites, the 'feminine' and 'masculine' valencies differentiatedly
present thematically in formational psychological personality,
so as to thuswise produce a symbolic 'intermediate type'
between the two biological sexes, an unnaturally 'round' *her-
maphroditus*. Better constituently effectuated through the first
ten alchemical operations, the luminous symbol and germinal
coniunctio of eminent twinship generativity wonderfully is now
more incarnately alive concordantly within him in a wholesomely intersexed sense of flexibly strong ego and well-felt
gay personhood morally, spiritually and governmentally
homosexually well nurtured deservedly and thus so suitably

capable functionally of healthily maturing object-love, and this subjective corporeal self-improvement is the life-elevating incestuous progeny of this concernedly growing man's dioscourian ritual initiation into the ancient mystical way of historically formative shamanism, the primordial human 'religion' by which, for vast millennia, the procreative 'civilizing power' of amative twinship generativity's energic evolutional viridity, the wondrously 'divine and creative nature of homosexual love,' fruitfully produced realizationally through succeeding fertile generations of similarly 'transformed' personalities, psychically-gynandromorphic shamans, the fecund 'children of the mind' that have blossomed contributively into the various religions, sciences, arts and civilizations of all humanity, and which has now generated in the contemporary personality achievement of linguistically-framed gay identity a commendable formation of authentically established individuality and sincere homosexual love of a politically-revolutionary nature authorizationally which can thus so, in turn, serve meaningfully as a much-needed 'forward force' transvaluationally for necessary human psychological growth more so in general emphoweringly, thereby satisfying an implicit ethical purpose farsightedly impelling the initial and continuing historical rise of the modern gay liberation movement to begin with morally, which is to deepen authentic personal actualization of the emancipatory Enlightenment promissory project irretrievably."

Here is an imaginative amplification that can prove quite evocatively stimulating if one contemplates achieving a good gay identity as provocatively embodying such significational import and visionary depth of valuable internal meaning.

On top of this, as I mentioned before, the entire *Rosarium* sequence encompasses twenty operational pictures that actually portray three transmuting cycles of elemental reformational growth, of which the first cycle produces the White or

Silver *Rebis* or magic hermaphrodite, the Empress of all honor, the second sequence renders the Yellow or Golden *Rebis*, The Emperor of all honor, and the third results in the Red or Ruby hermaphrodite, portrayed as a risen Jesus.

If we metaphorize the subjective achievement of a good gay identity to the elemental transformations culminating in the glorious Silver *Rebis*, as we have just looked at doing exemplificationally a moment ago, than what equivalent personality reformulations are similarly represented by subsequently gaining a Golden and then a Ruby state of valuable homosexual personhood?

Here we justifiably come to fair realms of gay fantasy stimulation and psychological possibility that are indeed metaphorically like inaugurally entering a long-denied and neglected storeroom of exquisitely jeweled preciousness, the most treasurable wealth of improvedly-refined homosexual subjectivity. In *The Uranian Soul* I comparatively consider the more-advanced forms of the alchemical *Rebis* to amplificationally represent or suggest two further recreations of estimable gay identity after its first victorious establishment, more advanced states of homosexual self-becoming advantageously attained through tackling, first, the problem of having a shadow after accomplishing a solid gay identity, which progresses to a fundamental encounter with the homosexually-organized, negative mother-complex so as to realizationally achieve a Golden Solar *Rebis*, which in turn leads to thorough encounter with the negative father-complex, culminating in final resurrection in a Glorified Body as the rubeous Red *Rebis*, which renders a still-better-personalized myth of meaning about what I figuratively likened to a homosexual bodhisattva of same-sex True Love enlightenmentally teaching about Ultimate Liberation.

Here is some of how *The Uranian Soul* analytically discusses the entire three-fold nature of that complete story told by the full twenty *Rosarium* pictures as amplifying the process of gay identity formation all the way:

"More inclusively regarding the entire alchemical opus of ably effecting a most-auspicious evolutionary gay existence revaluatively, what depthfully amounts symbolically to the personal actualization of an underlyingly-comprehensive, entelechical 'myth of meaning' numinously at organizational work determinationally in subjectively operational self-becoming homosexually undergone regenerationally, it is the thematic case that the laudable qualitative incorporation of the proudly distinguished White *Rebis* valuationally establishes in individually concretizing psyche amelioratorily the illustrious *unio mentalis*, the balmicly luminative 'mental union' manifested felicitously with the amative breath-buddy soul, on which sure mythic basis advancingly-modern gay identity in discerning ideological categorization is cohesively individually well shapefully founded compositionally in ongoingly-healthy homosexual feeling life well formulatedly received aromatically in mutually-mirroring linguistic comprehension, so as to successfully mediate coherently, reliably and accurately the adult ego personality effectively to social opportunities, challenges and demands. This more extravert-oriented stage of usefully-enlarged gay psychological growth, when satisfyingly-enough attained emancipationally, then, is to be subsequently followed developmentally by a second, 'centroverted' stage in the wholesome individuation process operationally occurring in appropriate improvemental response to the further obligating call of the self-realizing, archetypal Self, which is persistently autochthonously pulling on a growthfully-functional homosexual man circumstantially due in gay particular, it can be imagined, to his ongoing subjective metaphorical conditions of perpetually propulsive soul-twinship, its fundamental liberatory differentness from predominant reproductive heterosexuality, and the consequent crosswise gender involvement allegorically entailed by the childhood Uranian complex of incestuously falling in love with father and wishing to take mother's place.

"We then comparatively amplified the second ten *Rosarium* pictures to subsequently show the essential constitutional nature and valued substantive outcome possible to this further endogenous phase in the gay emancipatory individuation of primordial psychic energy, which enhanced compositional development itself fruitfully progressed through two narrative stages. In the first of these, representatively depicted in the seven consecutive pictures that follow the triumphant, autarkic White Rebis, we characterized a more purposeful 'introverting' of the gay identity formation process by which an established gay man more consciously 'comes out' substantificationally into the inner object world of his living subjective psyche through purposeful self-analysis of his still-discordantly gloomy Shadow side. In this again life-changing procedure, it is the mythically-storied case that the alchemical operations of the first luminescent cycle, the interplanetary mutational ascent reformulationally up the verdant Divine Ladder of utmost shimmering constitutional Perfection, are bravely thematically re-undergone experientially in a new initiatory cycle of the brightly-fiery haunting regenerationally by the homosexual soul so as to productively establish the epochal yellowing operation reformationally of commendable homosexual consciousness tangibly awakening redemptionally still specifically more clearly to itself knowledgeably within the interior subjective world thereby valuably so qualitatively expanding also, the royally clarifying *citrinatis*. By eminent evolutional way of this second infernal descent in our colorful allegorical adventure, prospectively-directed developmental issues pressingly present personally regarding the retrospectively-shaped Shadow and the brooding mother complex are effectively psychologically worked through sufficiently such that, in liberatory consequence, vibrant unknowing projections of the centrally animative soul are meaningfully reclamationally withdrawn back into the self-reflective psyche enough to consequently congeal there the quickened glowing *caelum*, the 'flesh and blood' equivalent to the sure *unio mentalis* as a psychically-embodied relational being manifestly recognized more directly within the dimensional subjective universe. Delightfully with this fresh manifestation, the now-dead White Rebis is corporeally reborn finely well transformed constitutionally, as the now-golden Solar Rebis of the greaterly triumphant Emperor of All Honor, in what then figuratively amounts to a glorious reparative reconciliation of needful son with good godsend father, thus satisfactionally gaining a second pivotal step toward successfully reaching an aeonic maturational resolution of the primal contradictory themes of the foundational parental complexes and the inferior moral self as constituting determinative developmental issues set into dialectical play by an underlying homosexual 'myth of meaning' thereso realizationally coming into humanizational psychodynamic being, the soundly strengthening basis of a second worthy Uranian identity formulationally and a yet more-fully embodied and energizing experience impactfully of individually-treasured gay personhood valuationally better compositionally rectified reproductively, the shining aureate identity of qualitatively-expanded inner understanding lovingly gained incarnationally through formidable relational union expansively with the magnificent living *caelum* victoriously so heroically forged rejuvenationally, with the vivistic representative Initiate of sagacious Father Thoth, ancient Egyptian god of spiritual wisdom, as tangibly etheric companion and inspirationally present teacher munificently coagulated sweetly within increasingly capacious subjectivity well enhancingly gained via homosexually-trophic romantic entanglement facilitatedly partnered psychologically.

"By the expeditive route of sublime interactional intimacy with this enlightening *caelum* figure fulfillingly so marvelously accessibly produced in the subjective homosexual mind, a third cyclotronic development of enriching energic constitution can liberatorily then be consequently compositionally undergone redressingly in now engagementally working through, in remaining metaphorical turn, the resident father complex's still-terrible hurtfulness and unrelated-to primitive violence sufficiently to competently proceed realizationally farther incorporatively along our imagistic journey in good gay self-becoming, and thus another beneficial elemental ascent transmutationally up the reformatory Ladder is thereby well analogically undertaken in the final reddening operation, the most-so gemmy *rubedo*, that again more-advanced, libidinally empowering initiation renewingly in the awakened etheric Temple of the sagacious heartfelt Sorcerers. In this culminating emblematic procedure of best-refined subjective self-determination, according to our careful narrative allegory, mystically occurs renovationally the third luminescent apotheosis exquisitely of the amatively metamorphic soul to rectifyingly produce accomplishingly the pristine Red Rebis of encompassingly crowning union with the ultimate *unus mundus*, the beauteously universal World Soul. In this conglobatingly-climactic transformation resolutionarily to fullest qualitative subjective consciousness symphoniously, the mythical Primal Parents of one's personal origin are entirely well differentiatedly sublimed atoningly, and a yet finer ego-Self axis or spinal bond with the archetypal Self is incorporatively forged verdantly that actualizingly configurates an emotionally much-matured, scrupulously valuably-redeemed, and coherently responsibly-awakened personality recuperatively which is self-governingly wholesomely expressive morally and spiritually of the cornucopic bodhisattva figure, a particularly-luminous third gay identity equally both inner- and outer-oriented splendorously, through which sacral valuational redemption self-authorshipfully the blazing autonomous Christos gorgeously best prospectively freely operates feelingly and thoughtfully in singularly-incarnated, agential human form most tangibly, influentially and contentmentally toward universal psychological realization."

Now we have summoned some very interesting material for good gay active-imagination practice in regard to further struggles and possibilities of estimable valuational becoming as a meaningful homosexual person, thus demonstrating a Uranian psychoanalytic approach in the salubrious introverting service of gay psychological relations and healthful interior growth, here in this later part of my talk, specifically directed towards better engaging through apt Jungian methods the numinously-prospective aspects of treasurable same-sex-loving subjectivity. When such homosexual active-imagination practice is responsibly combined in proper proportion with relevant appreciation for learning to be honestly embodimentally in the psychological moment and authentically as such efficaciously addressing retrospective issues of the inferior shadow personality, an encompassing ideological and practical stance toward progressive gay living today has been methodologically established that not only answers the dual challenge posed to continued gay relevance by increasingly one-sided assimilationist success combined with persistent internalized homophobia, but does so in an expediting fashion which, as can be seen by the suggestive amplifications we have gone over tonight, perhaps possesses a useful actualizational possibility authorizationally of extraordinary valuational reach, a signature kind of humanely enspiriting extension for modern Gay Liberation all-too-much needed redirectively by a dilutionally integrating same-sex-loving minority and, more globally, by a badly stymied and self-defeating humanity altogether.

I hope that tonight's foray into moreso exploring the particular features of a contemporary Uranian psychoanalytic approach to better homosexual individuation as a progressive political act of bejeweling initiatory possibilities, has usefully added to the overall picture of "Gay Liberation at a Psychological Crossroads" which I have presented in the prior three installments, and that taken together, these four expeditionary considerations into the future of homosexual ideology and establishment of the Institute for Contemporary Uranian Psychoanalysis will help point the way to a more effectually gay-affirming answer than has previously been provided to the action-oriented humanistic question historically now opportunely being proffered of what lies beyond gay identity and equality for estimable same-sex-loving personhood, for our community, and for the entire world, presently and productively into eras yet to come. Thank you.

PERFECTIONIS
ostensio.

Gay Psychological Responsibility and Enhanced Gay Pride: Some Brief Remarks in Honor of Gay Pride Month 2009

Given on June 6 in Plummer Park, CA

I learned to take up better psychological responsibility for myself, and the signal importance thereof, in stages through a period of many years, and indeed, I feel that I am continuing to learn about it more to this day. What is curious in my case, is that I was set on this internal developmental course, and motivated to go through its various challenging phases, by homosexual love, or at first, more properly speaking, by what I shamefully felt was the rising pubescent "problem" of my being wholly homosexually oriented and thus profoundly "diseased" and failed as a human being and as a future adult. So initially I certainly had no sense of gay pride, of an "affirmative" attitude toward being same-sex loving, much less one that was "gay-centered." Still, I was motivated by my terrible mortification about being homosexual to struggle with the issue, and this was the birth of my pursuit of better psychological responsibility for myself, which did simultaneously lead to gay self-acceptance and beyond.

To accomplish this sort of valuable personal growth, I underwent a series of stages in learning to accept myself as gay through being a psychological person, thuswise discovering the ethical and other important consequences arising therefrom which have led me to my present appreciation for these very pertinent matters, particularly in terms of fuller and more successful gay liberation. At first, I spent a year and a half through my initial efforts in extended psychotherapy trying to become straight, without any substantial success, but I did begin learning how to look for and at my personal psychology, what my own psychological qualities and issues might be, and how to engage them constructively through an exploratory handling of my dreams, fantasies, and forbidden thoughts. By way of this practical induction into psychodynamic "inner work," I eventually began to more clearly discern that my ongoing experience of spontaneously-upwelling homosexual desire and romantic yearning was not in fact about a negative, deficient, or otherwise "wrong" phenomenon, but rather it was homophobic condemnation which tried to make it so. And as I discovered this fresh re-evaluation, I felt a wonderful sense of manumissional release from much of that terrible shame and blame I was carrying about my same-sex orientation and thus my whole person, and I began to sense the first inklings of a new sort of inner understanding, connection, and integrity which seemed like such a terrific attitudinal and functional improvement as a meaningful human being over my prior ignominious situation that I felt justifiably impelled moreso in this enlightening direction with a growing surety which never once looked back in regret towards my previous wish to be heterosexual, or to merely "fit in," or to remain predominantly psychologically unconscious as our society then and now continues to promote and enforce.

Thus began my discovery of the magnificent and essential benefits to be gained by ongoingly learning to be self-honest, -sincere and -authentic to oneself through persistently practicing psychological self-awareness, -responsibility, and -engagement. That is, for example, if one is in important ways overly insecure, judgmental, or even impersonal or disembodied in how one feels about oneself subjectively, then it's a lot better to try to recognize that and deal with it, just as one would if there was some outer problem or concrete difficulty happening in one's literal life, and that in doing so, one may gain in self-growth, integrity, and other beneficial or even necessary subjective improvements. In applying this more multi-dimensionally enlightening sensibility by way of my own serious induction into ongoing inner work, I now slowly began to realize a truer level or degree of self-authenticity or quality of autogenous selfhood, what was trustably more really "me" or moreso "becoming myself" versus the opposite, and so at a certain point I then quit my straight therapist and instead began practicing other forms of psychotherapy that helped me become successfully same-sex loving, such as "humanistic," "gestalt," and "transactional analysis," which led to even better self-awakening and personality integration demonstrated in my life by coming out as gay, entering an academic Master's program in gay community and clinical psychology, and becoming a seriously-involved gay activist at the age of 21.

As I practiced and gained better training in this gay-affirmative psychological direction personally and profession-ally, I started to become aware that there were more pro-found aspects and valuations involved in being affirmatively same-sex loving than those I had been able to recognize so far, and in then undertaking a serious pursuit of better com-prehension in what seemed like a most intriguing direction, I felt myself metaphorically taken into a subjective initiatory quest of surprisingly major proportions during which I not only discovered a formulational way to combine gay libera-tion thought with classical Jungian psychology so as to better get at the numinous and transcendental qualities in being meaningfully homosexual, but was effectively brought into a revelatory confrontation with much more fundamental levels of personal woundedness and thwartedness from early expe-riences of narcissistic and homophobic parents and like-minded society than I had ever been able to access before, and through subsequently struggling with my own conse-quent resistances and overall ignorance, I discovered that by such persistent effort more profound integrative changes inside me were wrought which led to a wholly new appreciation for the resplendent domain of sacred enlightenment elationally resident within the luminous truth of eternal homosexual love, a thoughtful feeling regard of unexpected transcendent horizons. Thus I found myself imbued with a new kind of earned self-respect and answerable confidence about the wealthful validity of gay love and personhood, becoming all the more deeply persuaded as to the powerful association between committedly dealing with one's personal psychology and becoming better self-appreciatively same-sex loving and identified.

I am absolutely convinced through seeing my own good progress as well as the similar growth of many others over the decades, that improved self-esteem is created in the crucial developmental arena of personal self-integrity by accountably coming to see and better handle one's negative psychological issues and themes of woundedness, thwartedness, and other painful difficulties thuswise encountered in sensitively attending to the existential feeling or experience of oneself, no matter who you are. At the same time, if one is homosexual, coming into improved psychological self-acceptance and appreciation through systematic inner work will obviously enhance the presence and functioning of successful gay-identified personhood, thus contributing to the gay-specific tasks of healthy psychological healing from toxic homophobia and the satisfactional actualization of further valuable possibilities in being same-sex loving.

It seems to me that, as human cultural history well demonstrates, there are marvelous potentials in homosexual experience and gay identity of a sincerely awesome nature, a singular, rewarding nature of that special type requiring serious courage and effort to better realizationally attain, yet if today and into the future we do not reach for such

wealthful ambitions of gay self-enhancement and thus community progress, I fear that the lingering presence of poisonous internalized homophobia in noxious combination
with powerful assimilationist successes like legalized gay
marriage will so water down the ongoing meaning of gay
liberation ideology and practice as to render that concept
almost meaningless or irrelevant, thus continuing to stifle
not only the healthy growth of better-enhanced gay pride
and all the individual and collective benefits which would
arise therefrom, but especially as preventing any more-
serious efforts through this particular emancipatory route
to turn around that unconsciously addicted and lemming-
like system of power-mongering group mindedness which
is currently in charge of the human world overall and
thereso driving our so-called "sapient" species to the cliffs
of extinction. We humans need more psychological self-
consciousness and -responsibility as the functional key to a
fresh survival strategy on earth of better sustainable proportions, as a linchpin political attitude toward realistically actualizing a new and more-accurately democratic order of
interpersonal, societal, and global justice. And I am additionally suggesting that a practical appreciation for the great
moral and spiritual rejuvenations to be pridefully attained
in further gay self-realization through moreso authentically
facing one's wounded gay shadow psychologically can and
will bring a scope and scale of enhanced homosexual
integrity and delight deservedly manifesting that magnificent, glorious, and vital spirit of eternally-sourced provenance which, I would suggest, is behind the metaphor and
possibility of psychological self-relationship to begin with,
a spirit of same-sex love between equals unsurpassed not
only in its ability to contribute generally to changing humanity's current world prospects, but also most specifically in
its facility at enabling through maturational gay liberation an

accountable exemplification and radiant modeling of internally revalued personhood numinously possessed reparationally of a greatly-refined qualitative fulfillment, well politically-reorganized trustworthiness, and most richly-persuasive testimonial presence, a needed ethical presence which I believe is now becoming, at this time of historical juncture and opportunity, more tangibly achievable by pioneering way of all our sincerely concerted efforts at exploring and applying gay-centered psychological understanding. Thank you.

References

Blain, R. (2008, April 8). Follow your yellow brick road. *Frontiers, 26*(24), 52, 54.

Cass, V. C. (1979). Homosexual identity formation: A theoretical model. *Journal of Homosexuality, 4,* 219-235.

de la Huerta, C. (1999). *Coming out spiritually: The next step.* New York: Tarcher.

Duberman. M. (2008, September-October). Taking the 'cure' at Harvard in the 50's. *The Gay & Lesbian Review Worldwide, 15*(5), 28-29.

Edinger, E. F. (1972). *Ego and archetype: Individuation and the religious function of the psyche.* New York: G. P. Putnam's Sons.

Fabricius, J. (1976). *Alchemy: The medieval alchemists and their royal art.* Copenhangen: Rosenkild & Bagger.

Fone, B. (1980). *Hidden heritage: History and the gay imagination, an anthology.* New York: Avocation Publishers.

Gardner, J., & Maier, J. (1984). *Gilgamesh, translated from the Sin-leqi-unninni version.* New York: Random House.

Hannah, B. (1981). *Encounters with the soul: Active imagination as developed by C.G. Jung.* Boston: Sigo.

Johnson, T. (1999). G*ay Spirituality: The role of gay identity in the transformation of human consciousness.* Los Angeles: Alyson Publications.

Jonas, H. (1963). *The Gnostic religion: The message of the alien god and the beginnings of Christianity.* Boston: Beacon.

Kilhefner, D. (2006, Summer). Gay adults! Gay adults! Where are you? Trust the river of life. *White Crane, 69,* retrieved from http://whitecrane.typepad.com/journal/2006/07/don_kilhefner_g.html

Kilhefner, D. (2007, Spring). Night movies. Pay attention to your dreams...They are leading you somewhere. *White Crane, 72,* 29-30.

Kilhefner, D. (2008, September 9). Gay men and the great father-son wound: The inner work. *Frontiers, 27*(9), 60, 62.

Kilhefner, D. (2008, Fall). The gay community in crisis: Commentary on "Gay People at a Critical Crossroads: Assimilation or Affirmation" thirty years later. *White Crane, 78,* 13-16.

Kilhefner, D. (2009, January 27). The Radical Faeries at 30. *Frontiers, 27*(19), 51.

Lamy, L. (1981). *Egyptian mysteries: New light on ancient spiritual knowledge.* New York: Crossroad.

Mead, G. R. S. (1960). *Fragments of a faith forgotten.* Hyde Park, NY: University Books. (Original work published 1900)

Nimmons, D. (2002). *The soul beneath the skin: The unseen hearts and habits of gay men.* New York: St. Martin's.

Plato. (1956). *The works of Plato* (I. Edman, Ed.; B. Jowett, Trans.). New York: Random House.

Roscoe, W. (1996). Afterword. In H. Hay, *Radically gay: Gay liberation in the words of its founder* (pp. 331-354). Boston: Beacon.

Rogers, C. R. (1961). *On becoming a person: A therapist's view of psychotherapy.* New York: Houghton-Mifflin.

Smight, J. (Director), Isherwood, C. (Writer), & Bachardy, D. (Writer). (1973). *Frankenstein: The true story.* [Motion picture for television]. United States: Universal Studios.

Thompson, M. (Ed.). (1987). *Gay spirit: Myth and meaning.* New York: St. Martin's.

von Franz, M. L. (1980). *Projection and re-collection in Jungian psychology: Reflections of the soul* (W.H. Kennedy, Trans.). La Salle, IL: Open Court.

Walker, M. (1976). The double: an archetypal configuration. *Spring 1976,* 165-175.

Walker, M. (1980). *Visionary love: A spirit book of gay mythology and transmutational faerie.* San Francisco: Treeroots Press.

Walker, M. (1991). Jung and homophobia. *Spring 51,* 55-70.

Walker, M. (1994). *Men loving men: A gay sex guide and consciousness book.* San Francisco: Gay Sunshine Press. (Original work published 1977)

Walker, M. (1999). *The revolutionary psychology of gay-centeredness in men.* Los Angeles: Author.

Walker, M. (2008). *The Uranian soul: A gay-centered Jungian psychology of male homosexual personhood for a new era of gay liberation politics with universal implicational import.* Manuscript submitted for publication.

A Few Books on Jungian Psychology:

Johnson, R. (1986). *Inner work: Using dreams and active imagination for personal growth.* San Francisco: Harper San Francisco.

Jung, C. G. (1963). *Memories, dreams, reflections* (rev. ed., R. and C. Winston, Trans.). New York: Random House.

Jung. C. G. (1968). *Man and his symbols.* New York: Dell.

Singer, J. (1972). *Boundaries of the soul: The practice of Jung's psychology.* New York: Anchor/Doubleday.

A Few Books on Gay Liberation and its History:

Crompton, L. (2003). *Homosexuality and civilization.* Cambridge, MA: The Belknap Press.

Duberman, M., Vicinus, M., & Chauncey, G. (Eds.). (1989). *Hidden from history: Reclaiming the gay and lesbian past.* New York: Meridian.

Edsall, N. (2003). *Toward Stonewall: Homosexuality and society in the modern Western world.* Charlottesville, VA: University of Virginia.

Miller, N. (1995). *Out of the past: Gay and lesbian history from 1869 to the present.* New York: Vantage.

A Few Books on the Modern Development of
    Subjectivity:
Dunlap, P. (2008). *Awakening our faith in the future: The*
    advent of psychological liberalism. New York: Routledge.
Seigel, J. (2005). *The idea of the self: Thought and experiences*
    in Western Europe since the seventeenth century.
    Cambridge, UK: Cambridge University Press.
Taylor, C. (1989). *Sources of the self: The making of modern*
    identity. Cambridge, MA: Harvard University Press.
Zaretsky, E. (2004). *Secrets of the soul: A social and cultural*
    history of psychoanalysis. New York: Knopf.

About the Author: Mitch Walker, Ph.D., is a gay community activist, Jungian scholar, and homosexually centered psychologist currently living in Los Angeles. He was the first "out" gay writer to be published in the serious Jungian literature, with his groundbreaking paper on "The Double" in *Spring 1976.* He is the author of *Men Loving Men* (1977), *Visionary Love* (1980), *The Revolutionary Psychology of Gay-Centeredness in Men* (1999), and *The Uranian Soul* (2008). He is also co-founder of the Radical Faeries, Treeroots, and the Institute for Contemporary Uranian Psychoanalysis.

About the Publisher: Established in Los Angeles in 2005, the Institute for Contemporary Uranian Psychoanalysis is the world's first analytical organization to provide training, education, research, and publications dedicated to homosexually-centered psychological self-development as a principal route to the realization of gay peoples' fullest ethical, political, creative, and loving potentials. For more information, visit www.uranianpsych.org.